NOT
NORMAL

7 QUIRKS OF INCREDIBLE VOLUNTEERS

SUE MILLER & ADAM DUCKWORTH

orange

Not Normal: Seven Quirks of Incredible Volunteers

www.NotNormalBook.com

Published by Orange, a division of The reThink Group, Inc.
5870 Charlotte Lane, Suite 300
Cumming, GA 30040 U.S.A.

The Orange logo is a registered trademark of The reThink Group, Inc.

Other Orange products are available online and direct from the publisher. Visit our website at www.ThinkOrange.org for more resources like these.

ISBN: 978-1-941259-15-3

©2015 Sue Miller and Adam Duckworth

Lead Editor: Mike Jeffries
Art Direction: Ryan Boon
Cover Design: Hudson Phillips
Interior Design: Sharon van Rossum
Foreword: Reggie Joiner

Printed in the United States of America

First Edition 2015

3 4 5 6 7 8 9 10 11 12

12/01/15

CONTENTS

FOREWORD

So, you're a volunteer.

Maybe you're a brand new volunteer and you are in the first stages of this journey.

Or, maybe you have been volunteering for a long, long time and are leaving an amazing legacy.

Or, maybe you have been volunteering and love it so much you want to make a career out of it.

Or, you were a volunteer once and you decided it was time to hang it up.

Either way, you're not normal.

"Not normal," you say? What does that mean?

Well, normal means doing what's expected, what everyone else does. That doesn't apply to any of you.

You have signed up to do the unexpected. The not normal thing. You are a volunteer. You have chosen to do this crazy thing of helping someone else – for free.

Wherever you are in this journey, this book is for you. Volunteers who live out these quirky things soar in their roles, and get the most out of their experiences.

Our goal is to grow your quirkiness. We want to help you become even more not normal.

If we were honest with ourselves, most of us would say that we don't want to be just normal. We want more out of life, and we truly believe God has more for us than what we are currently doing. We wonder, "What if circumstances were different?" or "What if we hadn't made that one mistake?" or "What if life had taken a different turn twenty years ago?" If only that one thing was different, we could have something different than we have now.

The not normal difference happens when we engage with something bigger than ourselves. That's why in this book, Sue Miller and Adam Duckworth have unpacked seven principles – or "quirks"– that they have experienced during their time leading some of the nation's most innovative approaches to family ministry. Quirks are positive, unusual behaviors that spin into powerful impacts and unexpected results.

Sue and Adam are two of my favorite leaders. Individually, each one has extraordinary influence. But together, their combined voice quickly gets out-of-control quirky. The result? Some new ways of helping parents, small group leaders, volunteers and kids experience faith in a way that's not normal.

When we've watched people apply these principles and practices, we have seen them grow and lead in ways you wouldn't expect. Wherever you are in this process, we think you will do the same when you understand and apply these quirks.

After all, you're just not normal.

– Reggie Joiner

CHA

PTER

1

START SOMEWHERE

This first quirk is a fairly simple one, but one of the most meaningful if we are to begin living not normal lives. **Get started.**

Most of us start out really wanting to do something that matters with our lives.

Then we get busy. Then just when we can manage how busy we are, we get comfortable.

COMFORTABLE LIVING THE STATUS QUO

COMFORTABLE FOCUSED ON OUR OWN NEEDS AND INTERESTS

COMFORTABLE WITH OUR CURRENT ROUTINES

This all feels quite normal.

But along the way, every now and then, we live with a sense that something is missing. Something more important than all of this everyday stuff. Something much bigger. Something that's going to outlast our time on this planet.

Every single one of us dreams about giving ourselves to an important cause. We imagine how great it would be to change something in the world that would make life better for someone else. We long to give ourselves to something bigger than our own lives and interests.

Needs are all around us each and every day. Some of them are really big needs, and some are really small needs. Some of these needs happen at our churches, and some of them happen in our communities, and some happen in other countries. Some happen with people we know and some happen with complete strangers.

We want it. We think about it. But then we get stuck.

Why?

It's not because there aren't great causes to give ourselves away to — there are huge needs in our world pulling at us from all directions.

It's not because we don't have something to contribute — we have abilities that could help someone else.

It's not even because we don't have enough time (although we often say we don't). The truth is, we always find time to do what matters most to us.

So, what causes the stuck-ness?

IT'S BECAUSE THE NEEDS ARE TOO BIG.

IT'S BECAUSE THERE ARE TOO MANY TO CHOOSE FROM.

BUT MOSTLY, IT'S BECAUSE WE NEVER GET STARTED.

We are only one person. How much of a difference could one person make?

WE IMAGINE HOW
GREAT IT WOULD BE TO
**CHANGE SOMETHING IN
THE WORLD THAT WOULD
MAKE LIFE BETTER FOR
SOMEONE ELSE.** WE LONG
TO GIVE OURSELVES TO
SOMETHING BIGGER
THAN OUR OWN LIVES
AND INTERESTS.

It's absolutely overwhelming! How do you decide who to help? Where do you even begin? Way too much is needed to even make a slight dent in the world-changing arena.

So, because some of us can't figure out how to do everything some of us don't do anything.

We settle for what's normal.

But it doesn't have to be this way. There is a not normal life out there with your name on it.

> **THERE IS A NOT NORMAL MISSION THAT WILL CAPTURE YOUR HEART AND YOUR IMAGINATION.**
>
> **THERE IS A NOT NORMAL ORGANIZATION THAT CAN SHOW YOU KNOW-HOW TO CHANGE SOMEONE ELSE'S WORLD.**
>
> **THERE IS A NOT NORMAL LIFE FILLED WITH PURPOSE AND FULFILLMENT LIKE YOU'VE NEVER EXPERIENCED BEFORE.**

It's simpler than you think.

Which takes us back to Not Normal Quirk Number One… **take one small step and just start volunteering somewhere.**

INTERESTING APPEAL

Sometimes the quirky opportunity is right in front of you, and you just need to say yes to something that sounds good to you.

Callie worked in the corporate world as a very busy executive. Her time was swallowed up by work and family, leaving very little time for much else. But then her company threw a wrench in her well-ordered life by placing a volunteer opportunity right smack-dab in front of her.

It was an innocent gesture. A new initiative, if you will. Senior executives were going to let any director take their team on a volunteer adventure building houses in the southeast for one week of time with pay. They were convinced that great team building would happen as a result of their time away making them better work partners and more compassionate human beings.

Callie's team had been experiencing some corporate bumps and bruises lately, and their spirits were low. So, this idea appealed to her. She thought this might do them all some good. What did she have to lose?

So she said yes to her first experience ever as a volunteer, as simple as that. Callie rallied her team around the house building idea, and they made plans to give it a shot together.

The day her team arrived at the construction site they met other volunteers from across the country already there working. Things felt awkward at first, with folks on her team sensing they were out of their comfort zone.

Did they belong here?

What had they gotten themselves into?

But they were quickly absorbed into assigned teams with specific assignments, eventually finding their groove as time went on that first day.

Turns out, building a house is a lot of really hard work. Early mornings, long hours, lots of physical labor doing things they weren't used to day after day. Muscles were stretched, backs got stiff, and everyone had blisters and sore feet by day three.

But, the job site was a happy place. Music was playing, a few people were singing along out loud from time to time, and sometimes a few would dance with each for ten seconds when they passed. High fives were given whenever something was completed successfully. People joked and laughed freely with each other.

At the end of each exhausting day, the chief contractor would tell them what a great job they had done, listing all of the tasks that had been accomplished. He would end by giving them one new fact about the family they were building their house for to give them fresh perspective about what they were doing. People hooted and hollered after every new piece of information was shared, reminded that soon all of this was going to be worth it.

At night, Callie's teammates hung out to rehash their day. Often they belly-laughed really hard as someone shared the latest mishap that had happened. One of their favorite stories was about a team member who had installed a toilet for the first time ever, and as a known germaphobe had everybody rolling with his version of how he had gotten the job done. This team had moved beyond the work partner status, and had actually become friends who liked being together.

The showstopper moment came when all of the volunteers got to meet the single mom and her three children in person. She thanked each one of them so sincerely, telling them the many ways this house was going to change her family's future. There wasn't a dry eye in the place as she spoke.

They watched in awe when she was given the keys to her very first house.

Spontaneous cheers erupted from everywhere as she raised the keys up over her head and waved them in the air, unable to contain her joy.

In that moment, Callie felt something shift on the inside. Something new clicked into place. This was what had been missing in her life. This was the something bigger, something more important that she had been waiting to find.

THIS FEELING OF FULFILLMENT

THIS SENSE OF SIGNIFICANCE

THIS REALIZATION OF PURPOSE AND MEANING

She had tasted what this was like, and she wanted more. She wanted her family to experience what she had experienced. Callie wanted them to see and feel the difference they could make when helping someone else have a new beginning.

It was better than she had even imagined.

Callie had no idea where she would volunteer from here, but she knew she could no longer settle for less. She had to start living a not normal life.

Sometimes, an appealing volunteer opportunity is right in front of you and you just need to say yes. Other times, it may not be so obvious. You may want to ask yourself some questions to help you figure out what appeals to you. . . . .

The best way to make sure you're starting in the right way is to ask. . . . .

WHAT AM I GOOD AT?

WHAT DO I ENJOY DOING?

WHAT COMES NATURALLY TO ME?

God designed each one of us uniquely, and gifted us in different ways.

NO ONE CAN DO WHAT YOU CAN DO, NOR CAN THEY DO IT LIKE YOU WOULD DO IT.

NO ONE HAS THE HISTORY THAT YOU HAVE TO UNDERSTAND THE CONTEXT FOR WHY YOU WOULD DO IT.

NO ONE HAS THE DRIVE THAT YOU HAVE TO BE PASSIONATE FOR WHAT YOU ARE PASSIONATE ABOUT.

You have a unique contribution to make in order to make someone's world better.

Next, ask yourself what would you like to see change in this world.

WHAT MAKES YOUR HEART BEAT FASTER?

WHAT INJUSTICE MAKES YOU MAD?

WHAT DO YOU SEE ON THE NEWS AND YOU SAY, "I HAVE TO DO SOMETHING ABOUT THIS!"?

Not sure? Talk to someone in your local community about places to volunteer. Or, just Google "volunteering" and the name of your town. We think you'll find opportunities are everywhere!

In our opinion, local churches are great places to make a difference. We believe that the local church has something to offer the community that no one else can. By partnering with other key influencers, the local church can be an answer for all kinds of questions people are asking.

That's where we both decided to start volunteering.

See,

WE CAN'T STAND THE THOUGHT OF A GENERATION GROWING UP WITHOUT FAITH IN A REALLY BIG GOD.

WE CAN'T STAND THAT PEOPLE HAVE A NEGATIVE OPINION OF CHURCHES AND DON'T WANT TO BRING THEIR KIDS TO THEM.

WE CAN'T STAND THAT THE MESSAGE OF JESUS HAS BEEN HIJACKED BY PEOPLE WHO WEREN'T REPRESENTING HIM PROPERLY.

We couldn't be normal any more. We had to do something about it.

Okay, that's what fires us up. **Now let's focus on you.**

Think about the things that you already like to do, and find a place that is looking for something you are good at.

If you like to cook, join a cooking club that volunteers to make meals for those who need food brought in at your church. Volunteer at a local food pantry for an hour a week. Find a soup kitchen and show up there to help make meals and serve them to those who are in need.

If gardening is your love, volunteer on a team to make the grounds beautiful at your church, local school or community center. Investigate opportunities with nonprofits in your area and offer to care for their flowers, shrubs and grass.

If you like working on cars, find a group in your community who like the same thing and volunteer to work on cars for single mothers.

If technology is your thing, then check out the production team at your church to find out how you could put your skills to good use. You'll get to watch a lot of great programs come together, and put your gift to use at the same time.

Here's the good news. There is a place where you can use what you like to do as a volunteer to care for someone else.

VOLUNTEERING IS MEANT TO BE ENERGIZING.

VOLUNTEERING IS MEANT TO BE FULFILLING.

VOLUNTEERING IS MEANT TO BE ENGAGING.

Volunteering isn't meant to force you to do something you don't like to do. It is not supposed to be draining. You shouldn't feel like you gave a pint of blood every time after you volunteer.

So, try something that appeals to you, and just start somewhere.

Do something.

Take one small step and see how your life can be changed.

START AGAIN AGAIN

Some of you have tried volunteering somewhere, and had a really bad experience.

YOU TRIED IT, IT WENT BADLY, AND YOU QUIT.

YOU HAVE BEEN THERE AND DONE THAT.

END OF STORY.

The problem we have with the things we just mentioned is that they are so normal. (We know, we are saying that word a lot, but it's true.)

NORMAL PEOPLE GIVE UP TOO EASILY.

NORMAL PEOPLE DON'T TRY AGAIN.

NORMAL PEOPLE OFTEN CARRY A CHIP ON THEIR SHOULDER.

The problem with some of us is that we strive for perfection or we strive for immediate gratification. Now don't get us wrong, for perfection isn't a bad thing. However when starting to volunteer, don't try to find the perfect spot right away. It doesn't exist. There is no such thing out there as a perfect instant situation.

MAYBE MAKING COPIES WASN'T FOR YOU.

MAYBE YOU FOUND OUT YOU REALLY DON'T LIKE THIRD GRADERS.

MAYBE YOU UNCOVERED THAT DEALING WITH MIDDLE SCHOOL GIRL DRAMA IS MORE THAN YOU CAN HANDLE.

Here's someone who's singing your song…

One of our favorite characters in all of television history is George Costanza from Seinfeld. If you know anything about this character, you know that George is known for failed relationships, being fired from jobs, pretty much all around not having his life together. In one episode, George and his friends are volunteering at a senior citizen center over the holidays. The episode begins with George, Jerry and Elaine in a coffee shop discussing the longing they all have to invest in people. They talk about how they have this thing inside of them that they feel like they want to give back.

But on George's first visit with the senior adult that he is assigned to, the experience gets really rough. This isn't George's perfect spot. In fact, after the first visit with the senior citizen, George tells Jerry, "Yeah, I'm a great quitter. It's one of the few things I do well. I come from a long line of quitters. My father was a quitter, my grandfather was a quitter. I was raised to give up!"[1]

George Costanza is normal. Well, in many ways George Costanza is not normal, but not in the same way we are talking about.

Most of us don't like to admit it, but if we have a bad experience, our first instinct is to give up.

But wait a minute, have you ever had a bad experience at a restaurant?

MAYBE IT WAS A RUDE OR DISINTERESTED SERVER.

MAYBE THE FOOD WAS TERRIBLE.

MAYBE THE REVIEWS ONLINE WERE TOTALLY WRONG.

Whatever the reason, you walked out, and you were never going back there again.

Did that one bad experience cause you to stop eating out? Probably not.

We simply cross that restaurant off of our list and move on to another one that we end up liking much better. But we don't give up on every restaurant forever just because we had one bad experience, right?

THERE ARE DOCTORS WHO DON'T CLICK WITH US.

THERE ARE HAIRCUTS GONE AWRY THAT MADE OUR EARS STICK OUT AND LOOK HUGE.

THERE ARE LESS-THAN-STELLAR SOCCER COACHES.

THERE ARE GRUMPY STORE CLERKS WHO DON'T WANT TO HELP.

But that doesn't mean we give up. We look for someone new, and start over.

If you had a bad experience we want to challenge you to start again someplace new.

Make another choice.

Try something else under a different leader. Maybe, even probably, in the same place.

Get back in the game with more information than you had before. You now know a little bit more about what you don't want to do. You have the ability to make a more informed choice.

For some of you, starting somewhere means starting over again.

This time, make sure you like what you are signing up to do when you volunteer.

DON'T SIGN UP TO BUILD HOUSES FOR OTHERS IF YOU HATE CONSTRUCTION ZONES.

DON'T SIGN UP TO WORK WITH KIDS IF THEIR ENERGY STRESSES AND DRAINS YOU.

DON'T SIGN UP TO BE ON A CREATIVE TEAM WHEN YOU LIKE ADMINISTRATION INSTEAD.

DON'T SIGN UP FOR STUDENT MINISTRY IF YOU HATE EMOTIONAL DRAMA AND PROCESS.

DON'T SIGN UP TO WEAR A BEAR SUIT IF YOU ARE ALLERGIC TO FAKE FUR.

Ask the leader for more details about the role you are volunteering for. Find out how she/he leads volunteers. What can you expect in your role? Ask why this role is important. Find out what success looks like so you will know what a clear win is for you. Ask more questions this time. And then, start again.

YOU WERE MADE FOR THIS

We can't help but think about all of the reality television shows that have vocal auditions. We consistently see family members and close friends encouraging people to sing who have no business singing. Our favorite is after the pep talk right before the audition and the great expectation that the singer will perform well. Then the contestant walks in front of the judges only to sound like a tortured animal. The thought races through our mind, "Who in the world is encouraging this poor person to sing?"

Generally, the aftermath of this experience is entertaining to watch. The auditioning vocalist cries his or her eyes out and adds a few expletives and gestures as he or she exits the building in a reality-television storm!

You were made for this, they said. Not so much.

But each of us was made for something, usually something very specific, and it's okay to walk through a few different experiences to find what it is.

For me (Adam), finding what I was made for meant accidentally walking into the wrong office. I thought I was supposed to volunteer with high school students, but I walked upstairs instead of downstairs and ended up in the elementary director's office. After talking with the elementary director (who I thought was the high school director), I knew I was in the right place. Even though I walked into the wrong office to sign up for the wrong age group, I ended up in the right place working with the right group for me.

Every individual has a different door to walk through (even a wrong door that may end up being the right door), and volunteering is part of who we are.

EVERY INDIVIDUAL HAS A DIFFERENT DOOR TO WALK THROUGH (EVEN A WRONG DOOR THAT MAY END UP BEING THE RIGHT DOOR), **AND VOLUNTEERING IS PART OF WHO WE ARE.**

In the United States last year, **64.5 million people** showed up to make the world better for someone somewhere. That's a lot of not normal people like us!

The estimated worth of those volunteers is $22.55 an hour. **They did $175 billion dollars of actual work.** So many things in our world would not get done without the help of caring volunteers.

A third of those 64.5 million volunteers spent their time helping at a **religious organization**, with another 25.6 percent in education and 14.7 percent in community organizations

These are good places to start, but what is it that motivates us to volunteer in the first place to help someone else?

For that answer, we have to go back to how we were made.

WE WERE CREATED TO LOVE.

WE WERE CREATED TO GIVE.

WE WERE CREATED TO CARE.

WE WERE CREATED TO HELP OTHERS.

That desire was hardwired into our DNA by our Creator who designed us from the get-go.

One of the early leaders of the Christian faith advised us this way: "Each of you should use whatever gift you have received to serve others, as faithful stewards of God's grace in its various forms" (I Peter 4:10 NIV).

You see, God knew that if we only focus on our own interests, we could become selfish individuals who hold onto our material stuff way too tightly. An inward, insular focus leads to emptiness and selfishness.

You were made for so much more than that.

God wants you to really live – in a not normal way – differently than anything you have ever experienced.

When you deeply believe in what you are doing and want to do everything you can to help it succeed and move forward, amazing things start to happen.

Life starts delivering the not normal results we have all been longing for.

> **GREATER CONTENTMENT HAPPENS WHEN YOU REALIZE YOU HAVE ENOUGH "STUFF" ALREADY.**
>
> **DEEPER FULFILLMENT COMES WITH GIVING RATHER THAN GETTING.**
>
> **MORE PERSONAL VALUE COMES FROM DOING SOMETHING LASTING IN THIS WORLD.**
>
> **BETTER OUTLOOK COMES WHEN YOU VIEW YOUR STRUGGLES IN LIGHT OF THOSE YOU ARE TRYING TO HELP.**
>
> **INCREDIBLE JOY SURFACES WHEN YOU GET TO SEE SOMEONE ELSE SOAR BECAUSE OF YOUR EFFORTS.**

Who doesn't want that?

These things come only when we partner with God to take care of the people He loves. We just have to start helping someone else. Do something for someone else.

We don't have to worry about trying to do everything for everyone in order to make a difference in this world. That's His job. Not ours. Phew! Don't you feel better?

Take a deep breath. Now exhale.

All you have to do is just start somewhere.

SUE STARTED AND STOPPED
5 QUIRKY THINGS

1

FLYING LESSONS

I logged in six hours of flying time with an instructor, That's about the time I realized you really had to have science and math skills to learn this stuff. I have neither.

BEING A CANDYSTRIPER

I loved being a hospital candystriper when I was in high school. I thought I should go into medicine. Except that medical stuff made me queasy. It turns out that I just liked meeting the people as a candy striper, and delivering their flowers and presents.

5

22

2

KNITTING

All of my friends were into this, so I thought I would give it a try. It's fun, it's creative. You will love it, they said. After dropping stitch after stitch while knitting row after row, sweat pouring down my forehead as I tried to get this right, I decided this was the most exasperating activity I had ever tried to do. Just. Too. Much.

KICKBOXING

After years of high-impact aerobics, this class looked interesting and fun. A great stress reliever from real life. Loved the first class until the next morning. I could not get out of the bed. For three days. Oops! (Adam's response: "Sue Miller was a KICKBOXER!?!!)

3

COOKING LESSONS

I had dreams of throwing great dinner parties. I wanted to like cooking more than I did, which was not at all. Turns out that knowing more about HOW to cook didn't really make me like cooking any more than I did. Which was not at all.

4

SPINNING CLASS

I went with my wife once, told her she was out of her mind, and never went back.

WRITING A BOOK OF QUOTES

Some of the quotes I had were "Very few people are reasonable people" and "You can choose not to be offended." I bounced the quotes off my friend John and John replied, "This sounds more like an argument with your wife than a book of quotes." I quickly discontinued the project.

WATCHING "THE BACHELOR"

When the show went to two hours of content, I couldn't deal with the situational drama for that amount of time. Meanwhile, my wife sat on the couch with a box of tissues.

ADAM
5 QUIRKY THINGS
STARTED AND STOPPED

2

BLEACHING MY HAIR STARK WHITE

I did this for years and thought it was cool. But the process of the peroxide destroying my scalp became too much pain. Beauty hurts, but cool shouldn't have to.

3

COLLECTING THINGS

Addictive personalities can be dangerous, and I have one. I am a collector at heart. The problem is, if I start collecting something, I have to have every single thing that has ever existed. So in 2014, I made the decision I was going to stop being a collector--of anything. (Act now to see an amazing collection of my Vinylmations on ebay).

CHA

PTER

2

SMALL IS BIG

The second quirk that incredible volunteers live out is the belief that **the smallest things we do can have the biggest results. Not normal results.**

It starts by understanding that every…

CARD YOU SEND

PHONE CALL YOU MAKE

BIRTHDAY YOU REMEMBER

GAME YOU ATTEND

ENCOURAGING WORD YOU SAY

HAND YOU HOLD

OR TEAR YOU WIPE AWAY

can mean more than you could ever imagine.

These aren't the moments that are going to increase your bank account, get you a luxury automobile, or cause you to become the CEO of a major corporation. We think it is fine for folks who achieve that status, but the moments we are talking about help you achieve a different type of status. The not normal kind.

Our culture talks about that other kind of BIG all the time. The way it is highlighted in our world today, it's easy to believe those achievements will make our lives feel richer and more fulfilled.

That's the promise, at least, until you actually get all of those things and put your head on the pillow at night wondering why you still have that empty feeling deep down inside.

The answer you are looking for can be found in the quirky small things you do for someone else as you volunteer. They seem small and simple at the time, but definitely have the biggest return overall.

You know why?

Jesus gave us the answer to this. He taught that when someone needs your help to go one mile, you should go two miles instead. He wanted us to go the extra mile. Unconditionally. We do this not because we have to, but because we want to. Not because of a paycheck, but with no expectations of anything in return.

THAT'S WHEN PEOPLE'S JAWS DROP.

THAT'S WHEN THEY DECIDE TO COME BACK TO YOUR CHURCH AGAIN.

THAT'S WHEN THEY WONDER ABOUT WHY YOU DO WHAT YOU DO.

That's when people decide to ask some important questions like

WHO MOVED THAT PARKING CONE SO I COULD GET OUT OF THE RAIN MORE QUICKLY?

WHY DID SOMEONE SEND MY CHILD A CARD ON HER BIRTHDAY?

WHO ARE THOSE PEOPLE WHO LOVE MY SPECIAL NEEDS SON FOR FREE?

WHICH OF THESE PEOPLE WAS NOT NORMAL ENOUGH TO VISIT MY DAD IN THE HOSPITAL?

HOW IN THE WORLD DO THESE PEOPLE GET UP AT 6 A.M. TO SET UP A STAGE?

WHO FOLDED ALL THESE PROGRAMS SO I COULD KEEP UP WITH AN UNFAMILIAR SERVICE?

WHO GIVES UP THEIR WEEKEND TO SERVE AT A SHELTER FOR HOMELESS MOMS?

We heard this quote recently, "When you do the small things right, big things happen." So many of us want to engage in something bigger. To do that, we need to first understand that going the extra mile in the small things is the pathway to making the big, not normal results happen.

MESSY SMALL

Whenever volunteers sign up for a particular initiative, they have a picture of how things will go. If you're the parking lot greeter, you know where the orange cones are, until it turns out someone moved them so they could be used for a message illustration. Or you come in on Thursday to fold the worship programs and find out the folding machine makes that perfect fold look like an origami circus. You offer to run tech for the college ministry, but find out too late that the simple sound board has more levers and latches and twirly things than the SpaceX lower-orbit shuttle.

Or take someone who signs up to lead a small group for kids or teenagers. First, we'll follow this curriculum lesson agenda. We will talk about these discussion questions. We'll do this activity or game together. Next, everyone will share how their week went so we can support each other.

We'll end on a positive note and finish with a prayer tying up everything we've talked about together. Sounds right, doesn't it?

But then, life gets messy. A rogue wind blows into someone's life around your circle and knocks them flat when....

AN ILLNESS SURFACES

SOMEONE GETS A FAILING GRADE

ONE PARENT FILES FOR DIVORCE

A PLAYER DOESN'T MAKE THE TEAM

SOMEONE GETS DUMPED

A CAR ACCIDENT HAPPENS

A SENIOR DOESN'T GET INTO HER FIRST, SECOND OR THIRD COLLEGE CHOICE

FAMILY IS MOVING ACROSS THE COUNTRY

SOMEONE HAS AN EATING DISORDER

A BULLY EMERGES

Times like these bring with them the unexpected, the unthinkable, and sometimes even the unimaginable. The darkness that comes in these moments can swallow a person up, making it impossible to see how to move forward.

THE WIND IS TOO STRONG.

THE CIRCUMSTANCES ARE TOO COMPLEX.

THE OBSTACLES ARE TOO BIG.

These moments can bring pain and sorrow, but they also bring a unique opportunity to put the agenda aside and demonstrate what unconditional love in action looks like instead. These are teachable moments....ones that should be seized by small group leaders. When handled wisely

THESE MOMENTS CAN BRING PAIN AND SORROW, BUT THEY ALSO BRING A UNIQUE OPPORTUNITY TO PUT THE AGENDA ASIDE AND **DEMONSTRATE WHAT UNCONDITIONAL LOVE IN ACTION LOOKS LIKE INSTEAD.**

and lovingly, these moments can bring joy that is unlike anything you've ever experienced. It happens when a not normal volunteer decides to love someone else just the way they are, mess or no mess. It happens when an incredible someone reaches out and cares about the big and small things in the quirkiest of ways.

This is a person who can….

LISTEN WITH YOU

CRY WITH YOU

DOUBT WITH YOU

ENGAGE WITH YOU

AND LET YOU KNOW THAT NO MATTER WHAT YOU'VE DONE, YOU WILL ALWAYS HAVE A PLACE AT THIS TABLE.

No matter the mess, these volunteers choose to stay in it with kids. They won't let teenagers give up on themselves. And over time, they gently help pull them back to their feet.

Or you stay at the sound board. Or you unfold and refold and fold again. Because you know it's not about the thing, it's about the people you're doing the thing for. So in good times and difficult times, you're there.

When a volunteer goes beyond what's normal and shows that kind of love for someone else, then joy can make its way into the darkness and turn on the light. Fresh opportunities emerge to show that God's love is for real, and He can be trusted. No Matter What.

A wise writer once said, "Weeping endures for a night, but joy comes in the morning" (Psalm 30:5).

Some of that joy is present only because of you, the volunteer. You usher it in when you show up and love those you're

NO MATTER THE MESS, THESE VOLUNTEERS CHOOSE TO STAY IN IT WITH KIDS. THEY WON'T LET TEENAGERS GIVE UP ON THEMSELVES. **AND OVER TIME, THEY GENTLY HELP PULL THEM BACK TO THEIR FEET.**

serving in the middle of their darkest night. Joy comes as you walk alongside them when they need you the most.

Not normal 25-year-old Haley knew about stuff like that because it had happened to her. That's what motivated her as a small group leader for the high school girls she cared about. These girls were now in their junior year. Haley met these girls as freshmen, and over the previous two years they had done sleepovers, movie nights, late night pizza, concerts and lots of coffee talks. They had weathered their fair share of relational drama along the way, but Haley continued to believe the best about each one of these girls.

She was passionate about giving them a safe place to process life and their faith each week. She remembered how critical these years are in the fight to make faith your own. Haley only had one non-negotiable: to be the kind of friends who love each other no matter what.

In November, that got put to the test by an event that ended up changing all of them in the very best way.

It started on a rainy Tuesday night during small group in Haley's living room. While snacking on popcorn and Diet Cokes, the girls took turns updating each other on their lives. Only Lindsey was left. She seemed unusually hesitant to talk, almost like she didn't want to. She started out slowly, struggling to get the right words out.

Finally, Lindsey just blurted it all out. "I need to tell you that a few of months ago, I made a big mistake, and now my life is a total wreck. This week I found out that I'm three months pregnant."

Big tears started rolling down her cheeks as she continued to share her story. You could have heard a pin drop in that living room. Every girl around the circle was feeling Lindsey's pain. No one dared to move. She completely broke down when she talked about how she had let her parents down. They were furious and disappointed. Neither of her parents went to church, but they knew that their daughter did. They thought that with all of that church-going surely she would know better.

Lindsey felt like such a failure.

HER BOYFRIEND WAS TERRIFIED AND DISTANT.

HIS PARENTS WANTED TO BLAME HER FOR WHAT HAPPENED.

THINGS WERE SUCH A MESS.

How had she let this happen? Everyone was mad at her. Her life was ruined forever, she was sure of it.

And then she just sat there and sobbed, no longer able to keep the pain in.

One by one, her friends got up and moved toward her until she was surrounded on all sides. One after another they hugged her. Most of them were crying too. Haley gently told Lindsey that her life was not ruined. In a comforting way, she explained that Lindsey had made a mistake, and things were going to be different now, but God still loved her and had a future for her.

Haley told Lindsey something that changed her perspective. She said, "God loves to give second chances when we make a mess of our lives; it is His specialty."

Bottom line, God wasn't giving up on her, and neither were they. No matter what. The girls talked about that for a few minutes, and then they prayed authentic, desperate prayers for Lindsey. Lindsey confessed to God that she had made a really bad choice, and asked for His forgiveness.

She wanted a second chance.

She didn't know what to do next and asked for His help.

God did something special in the group that night. A connection formed between them that was deeper than it had ever been before. Lindsey was not going to walk through this alone. They were going to do this together. The entire point of why a small group exists was realized in this exact moment and it changed everything in that group in a drastic and radical way.

For the next six months, Haley and that circle of girls loved Lindsey in a myriad of small ways, making things up as they went along. They took turns texting facts about how her baby was developing each month. They probably used up every fun emoticon available to make her smile. They sent song videos to make her laugh.

Not only did they show up in the small moments for her, they showed up to mark the big moments, too. Haley drove them to Lindsey's doctor's office so they could hear the baby's heartbeat for the very first time with her and her mom. It was such a moment that a party broke out in the room that made everyone in the lobby wonder if Lindsey was having septuplets! They were there when the doctor announced that the sonogram showed the baby was a girl. They screamed again, and once again the lobby of the office shook in fear. The girls walked out with pink feather boas wrapped around their necks that day. The small group threw her a pink glam baby shower with style and flair, truly a one-of-a-kind event. They invited both moms and entertained them thoroughly.

When baby girl made her way into the world, Haley drove all of the girls to the hospital to visit Lindsey and see her brand new baby. Both moms were already there and warmly welcomed them in to see the newly arrived, seven-pound miracle.

The joy in that room was obvious. . . . .

UNLIMITED SMILES

OVER-THE-TOP LAUGHTER

PLAYFUL TEASING

NONSTOP JOKING

PINK, WHITE AND GOLD BALLOON BOUQUETS, AND PIZZA BROUGHT IN FROM THEIR FAVORITE RESTAURANT.

The entire small group was over-the-moon happy for Lindsey.

One of the girls made a photo book of pictures taken over the past six months to chronicle their story together. Inside, each one had written a note to Lindsey about how they had been impacted and what they had learned while walking through this with her. The very last page had babysitting coupons so Lindsey would know her friends weren't walking away anytime soon. After all, next year they were going to be seniors and would rule the school.

Haley, her small group leader, had one last surprise. She dramatically revealed a hot pink glam onesie that said "NEWEST MEMBER" on it. She wanted Lindsey to know that her baby was welcome anytime in their small group. That's when Lindsey's mom totally lost it and had to leave the room.

WHO WERE THESE PEOPLE WHO LOVED HER DAUGHTER THIS MUCH?

WHY WOULD THEY DO ALL OF THIS?

WHAT WAS IN IT FOR THEM?

Lindsey's mom wondered about God and the people from this church that her daughter had been attending the past couple of years. The girls had already invited her to attend the Baby Dedication Celebration coming up in a couple of months. Maybe she would go. . . . . just for the baby's sake, mind you.

This story had started with darkness, despair, and failure. But six months later, forgiveness, hope and joy had crashed the party. They had been escorted in through the many small quirky ways that Halley and her friends showed God's love to Lindsey.

Unconditional love. This group learned how to love each other no matter what.

Free. This small group had no expectation of getting anything in return.

Active. These girls showed their love in very tangible ways.

Here is the question we ask you about these small things: Was it a big deal?

FOR LINDSEY?

FOR LINDSEY'S FAMILY WHICH DOESN'T GO TO CHURCH?

FOR HER BOYFRIEND'S FAMILY?

FOR HER NEW BABY GIRL?

IN GOD'S EYES?

Yes, messily so.

THOUGHTFUL SMALL

Often when volunteering, we get the opportunity to impact someone by seizing an everyday moment in time and doing something thoughtful to serve them in some way. The reason we impact them so significantly is because our actions show how deeply we care. We exceed their expectations, often surprising the daylights out of them in an unforgettable way.

It's fun, because we often leave them in a quandary trying to figure out why anyone would do this for them? It's not normal.

Why would someone care this much?

This kind of moment leaves everyone wanting to know more about why we volunteer, and wanting to know more about the God we are doing it for. It's the impact that comes with the extra mile.

There is an everyday simplicity that comes with being thoughtful. It's rarely complicated. Thoughtfulness can be as simple as greeting someone at the door, remembering a parent's name, or knowing a teenager's favorite coffee. This kind of kindness lets someone know that you value them, that they are important to you.

Here's how an opportunity unfolded on a Sunday morning in a preschool environment not too long ago.

Anyone who has spent time with preschoolers knows that each one has a certain something they cannot live without. (Well, there are probably many things that they can't live without, depending on the child.) But for two-year-old Landon, it was a midnight blue, soft and fuzzy blanket.

His mom usually didn't let him bring it INSIDE to church, but this time she made an exception. He was just getting over an ear infection and refused to go anywhere without his special blanket. So Landon checked into the twos room with it draped around his shoulders like a cape. He was happily scooped up by his small group leader, Jan, a not normal volunteer. She noticed his cool blanket right away. He showed it to her, and even let her feel how really awesome it was.

Landon clutched his blanket all through activity time, large group and small group. He was happy and attentive sitting next to his good friend, Steven. All in all, a happy camper. Which, if you know anything about preschoolers, is unheard of for one getting over an ear infection. When he left his room, he left waving to everyone, his blanket in tow.

After all the children had been picked up, the volunteers were hanging out catching up. They were surprised to see Landon's mom, Sarah, come bursting back through their door. Slightly panicked, she asked if anyone had seen Landon's blanket. Seems he didn't have it when she buckled him into his car seat and he was having a major meltdown.

Technically, this group of volunteers was off the clock. But Jan and several others jumped to their feet, accepting the missing blanket mission. They formed a plan and ran off in different directions, assuring the mom that they would search everywhere. Jan told Sarah to take her kids home and wait for her call.

Thirty minutes later, the midnight blue treasure was found. Somehow it had been dropped in a hallway, swept under a stack of chairs and carried into another room. Jan called Sarah, then jumped into her little white car and tore out of the parking lot. Jan was only 18 years old, but she knew you don't mess around when it comes to preschool matters of the heart. Landon was watching out the front window when Jan walked up the sidewalk waving his blanket so he could see it. That red, tear-streaked little face broke into a smile that could have lit up Chicago.

A grateful mom opened the front door and tried to thank her. But honestly, no one could hear anything over the exuberant two-year-old yelling "My blankie!! My blankie!!" while running full-force toward Jan.

Jan scooped him up and wrapped him in his blanket. They hung out for a few minutes and then it was time for Landon to go take a nap. Jan left admitting that she was going home to crash on her couch too.

No one is really sure who needed the rest more, Jan or the two-year-old.

Both had a pretty big morning.

Let's unpack this for a moment...

How big a deal was it for Jan to go beyond her normal serving responsibilities that day? She was thoughtful in the quirkiest ways doing things that she didn't have to do. It would have been easy for her to walk out of the church on that given Sunday, get into her car, and not give this blanket a second thought. But she didn't do that.

How big a deal is it that Sarah, Landon's mom, decided to join the preschool team because she was so impressed by the way this situation was handled?

How big a deal is it to communicate to a two-year-old that you care about them?

How great do you think Jan felt when she put her head on the pillow to go to sleep that night?

That is exactly what we are talking about. It's not at all normal. It is a really big deal.

Small is big.

LIFE-CHANGING SMALL

You might be wondering how much time it takes to serve as a not normal volunteer. It's actually less than you would think (assuming you don't have too many missing blue blankets).

We recently came across an article about the Six Secrets you can learn from the happiest people on the planet. (We don't know why they didn't ask us to give our secrets. After all, we are two of the happiest people we know.)

People who get the most out of their serving serve an average of two hours a week.

Every week.

They consider helping others to be high on their list of what makes them feel fulfilled. They like being part of something bigger than their own lives so they choose to show up and give back making someone else's life better.

It doesn't take a huge amount of time to make a big difference. Maybe just two hours. What else could you possibly do in just two hours that would change so many lives?

See, lives can be changed in many ways…

THOUGH CONVERSATIONS

THROUGH OPPORTUNITIES

THROUGH RELATIONSHIPS

THROUGH ACTS OF SERVICE

THAT IS EXACTLY WHAT WE
ARE TALKING ABOUT. IT'S
NOT AT ALL NORMAL.
IT IS A REALLY BIG DEAL.

Regardless of what you do, it is important to understand that it doesn't take a lot of time or a lot of effort to get involved in something that could change the trajectory of someone's life forever.

There is a guy we know named Steve. Steve started out as a greeter at the children's ministry entrance at one of our favorite churches.

Each week, Steve would stand outside the doors and welcome families as they arrived. He would help new families with the registration process and even walk them back to their rooms so they wouldn't have any trouble finding them. He took pride in that. Talk about a not normal volunteer!

Steve would always look for this one particular family. It was a mom and two sons, twins named Chester and David. Steve would always be the guy who would high five the boys and engage with them in some conversation about basketball, superheroes, or how they were doing in school. Steve knew they played basketball because oftentimes Chester and David would come in to church with their jerseys on because they had games right after church was over.

After Steve had gotten to know the family for about a year, one day the mother came in kind of troubled. Steve talked with her and found out Chester and David's father ran off when the boys were infants, and their mother has been raising them by herself ever since. The boys were beginning to ask questions like…

"The other kids have dads, Mom. Where did our dad go?"

This broke their mother's heart. She didn't know what to say or what to do. Frankly, Steve didn't either. But Steve did do something, the only thing that he could do in that situation. Steve asked if he could come to the twins' basketball game sometime. He didn't have an answer for the difficult questions being asked, but he knew he could give a little bit of his time and he did.

Chester and David were so excited that Steve, a guy who they knew from church, decided to cheer them on. And their excitement translated to Steve and he decided to take another volunteering step in response to that. He became even more not normal!

Steve signed up to be a small group leader with the age group that Chester and David were, and he began investing in their lives. This family was changed in significant ways because Steve decided to do just a little more.

Is this a big deal? We think so.

Small really is big.

Life-changingly so.

"A SMALL MEETING WITH A BIG FUTURE" (ADAM AND SUE'S STORY)

What if I (Adam) told you that one simple small conversation led to this book being written? It was the summer of 2006 and Sue Miller was doing a speaking engagement in Toledo, Ohio. My hometown was about a mile north of Toledo across the Michigan border, in a place called Temperance. Sue was doing speaking engagements on children's ministry, and "making Sundays the best hour of every kid's week." Sue coined that phrase years ago when she was directing the children's ministry at Willow Creek Community Church in the northwest suburbs of Chicago. That phrase has revolutionized the children's ministry world from the inside out. More people know it, more people remember it, and more people use it than any other phrase in the history of children's ministry! I love it, and I'm so glad I was introduced to it when I was.

But let me back up. I didn't really want to go to Sue's event. It's not that I didn't want to go to hear Sue speak, but I had recently taken over the children's ministry department at my home church and I had taken over from my old boss. My old boss was extremely successful and I admired her greatly. She was extremely organized and taught me so many things that I needed to learn about my future in managing leaders, managing volunteers, and navigating family situations. But the timing of her transition made for an awkward situation and, even though we didn't have any tension between us, showing up at the same conference was going to be beyond my comfort zone. So I almost talked myself out of going to the event.

Fears and anxieties aside, I decided to go. I'm glad I did because one small conversation changed my life forever. It convinced me of what we're trying to convince you, that small really is big.

If you know anything about Sue Miller, you know that you could take the combined energy level of one city block of any city in America and it probably would pale in comparison to the energy and passion that this one woman has. It's contagious. I love being around her, because it inspires me and excites me to do what I do better.

After Sue wrapped up speaking on that day, there was a line of folks waiting to speak to her. The line was so long that I almost decided not to wait. But, I did.

I approached Sue, we exchanged pleasantries and I talked to her a little bit about what I do. I told her that I was a young leader ready to knock it out of the park in kids ministry. I also told her how inspired I was by that phrase that she had coined about making one hour on Sunday the best hour of every kid's week. We talked and laughed about the things we loved about ministry. We had a lot in common for sure. Sue told me to keep growing as a leader. Months later, Sue volunteered to do something based on our conversation. Something she didn't have to do. Something that changed my life forever.

It was around this time that Sue Miller partnered up with Reggie Joiner and they both began working around this cause that we all now know called "Orange." Sue went to Reggie and said "I met this guy in Ohio, and he's so passionate that we have to have him on our team!"

That conversation led into a future that I could have never imagined: speaking, traveling, meeting with leaders (and now getting to help write books like this one!).

Did you ever think that one small conversation, one small decision, one small step of faith could change your life? Well I'm a living, breathing example that it can happen.

That's why we believe that small is big. We believe the same will be true for you as a not normal volunteer.

Think about it. A chance encounter led us to write these words down on these pages together, today.

What might happen to you if you believe that small is big?

5 SMALL THINGS
SUE DID

1 HIRED SOMEONE TO CLEAN MY HOUSE

I love coming home to a clean house. This was a difficult decision for me because I didn't want to be like one of "those people" who couldn't clean her own house! After I got over that, I realized that folks who clean houses need an income too. When you are working all day long, there is nothing like coming home to a spotless place.

TAKING A WALK OUTSIDE EVERY DAY 2

This is something that is simple, yet very powerful. Spending time out in nature fills me up and gives me time to think. If you have a moment to clear your mind, with no distractions, you can hear the sounds of nature, whether that is water flowing, the birds, or even wild animals. Taking a moment to do this made a big difference for me.

SAYING NO MORE OFTEN 3

Saying no is way more difficult than saying yes. Saying no causes me to slow down, and to think about what I would like to get involved with. I decide each season what I am going to focus on, and turn most everything else down. Less hurry. More intentionality.

4 LISTENING TO WORSHIP MUSIC

I feel closest to God when listening to songs that center my mind on how great He really is. I do this in my car on my way to work and it fills me up and gets me ready for any challenge that comes my way during my day. It also causes me to reflect on the past when I hear certain songs. The memories that flow through my mind of my early days in ministry do amazing things for my spirit.

THAT MADE A **BIG** QUIRKY DIFFERENCE

SURROUNDED MYSELF WITH JOYFUL, HAPPY FRIENDS WHO ARE FUN 5

About fifteen years ago, I made a conscious decision that I did not want to surround myself with negative people any longer. The difference that this made in my life was huge. It was like a weight was lifted off of my chest, and I have never looked back (even though sometimes they are chasing me.)

5 SMALL THINGS ADAM DID

1 STOPPED EATING FRENCH FRIES IN THE SPRING

This might sound weird, but it actually started around the liturgical tradition of "lent." Now, I am not Catholic, nor am I traditional, but this idea of sacrificing something intrigued me. So each spring I give up potatoes for approximately two months. It might not sound like much, but a few years back it kickstarted my journey to losing 50 pounds, and I've never put it back on.

SUBSCRIBED TO A MEN'S FASHION MAGAZINE 2

Three years ago, I was wearing my board shorts, a t-shirt, and a vest, and thought I looked good. Nothing could have been farther from the truth. Based on some advice I received from a good friend, I knew I had to change my ways, so I subscribed to Details Magazine. Now, you will see me in clothes that fit properly, many checked shirts, and an occasional blazer. The difference is stylishly substantial.

3 RUNNING

This isn't that small of a thing. This actually takes a lot of time and a lot of dedication. And, I hate it. There is literally nothing that I dislike more than running. It is exhausting. But, I know that for me to stay in shape long-term and to have a healthy life, exercise is essential to the process. I feel better about myself after every run I go on.

THAT MADE A BIG QUIRKY DIFFERENCE

TAKING B-COMPLEX VITAMINS

4

I was low on energy one day and someone said to me, "Rather than get another cup of coffee, start taking B-Complex vitamins. They help immensely with your energy level." I started, and I couldn't agree more. I take one when I get up each morning and it livens me up in fairly short order.

GOT MY FINANCIAL HOUSE IN ORDER

5

This is the largest small thing that I have ever done. It is also the most important. When Katelyn and I got married, we were in a fairly decent amount of debt and knew that to live a better life, we would have to get out of it, and that is what we did. When we paid off our debt it was the most freeing moment in the history of my entire life, and we have never looked back.

CHA

PTER

3

The third quirk is this: **Investing more not less for a bigger return.**

So, still tracking with us so far?

You're definitely ready to go bigger, in a not normal way, beyond what's expected.

But now you probably have some practical questions like…

HOW MUCH TIME ARE WE TALKING ABOUT?

AND HOW OFTEN ARE WE THINKING ABOUT?

CAN I STILL OWN A PET IF I AM GOING TO GIVE UP THIS MUCH OF MY TIME?

These are the right questions to wrestle with. Well, maybe not the last one. (Or maybe so…Adam just got a miniature goldendoodle named Dottie.)

The answer is a game-changer for every volunteer, more important than you would ever imagine.

You see, most of us start with a minimal commitment. That's the normal way to do things.

We like to put our toe in the water to check things out first.

We plan to serve occasionally, in case it's lame.

We want to be able to get out of dodge quickly if things go south.

It's okay to start there. The problem is most of us don't ever go beyond that first step. We volunteer like we are renters, not owners.

My wife and I (Adam) are currently renting an apartment. I've wanted to paint the walls ever since we moved in six years ago. The walls are hideous brown but my wife, Katelyn, refuses to paint. In fact, she doesn't want to do anything that would "up" the look of the apartment. It could be flooring, wall colors, bathroom fixtures or lighting. It doesn't matter what it is, she isn't doing it! It isn't the money, or the color. It is the fact that she doesn't want to put any more effort into something that isn't hers. This building is owned by someone else and we will see no return on any sort of investment we would make into this property. She is a renter of this property, and her attitude toward the apartment reflects that of most renters.

Renters only want to invest a little because....

RENTING IS TEMPORARY

IT'S PROBLEM-FREE

LESS COSTLY

A SHORT-TERM COMMITMENT

MOST OF US START WITH A
MINIMAL COMMITMENT. . .
IT'S OKAY TO START THERE.
**THE PROBLEM IS MOST
OF US DON'T EVER GO
BEYOND THAT FIRST STEP.**

Like Katelyn, most renters don't plan to do more than just pay the rent. They didn't sign up to fix anything, care about the lawn or make a strong connection to the neighborhood. If there's some trash on the sidewalk, they will simply walk around it, wishing someone "in charge" would pick that up. Renters aren't planning to add value to whatever they're renting. After all, this is not their place.

Have you ever rented a car? We do, a lot! When you travel like we do, it is the simplest way to get from place to place. Sure, you could take a bus or walk, but you don't have control of your own destiny like you do when you have your own car.

We love being at the rental car counter and the person at the counter offers us insurance. What a scam! Yeah, let me give you $39.99 per day only to have my deductible go up when something happens, with the company sending out another bill indicating that "this claim is not resolved." It isn't worth it. The rental car agent will say to us, "If you get the insurance, you can literally total the car, bring it back, and walk away clean!"

Think about this for a second, you would never do that to your own car. If you have a car you probably take some sense of pride in the vehicle that you drive. You probably. . . . .

KEEP IT CLEAN ON THE INSIDE.

KEEP IT CLEAN ON THE OUTSIDE.

CHANGE THE OIL EVERY 2,500 MILES.

GET IT WAXED EVERY NOW AND THEN.

There is a sense of pride in this vehicle, because you OWN it. Even if it isn't paid for in full, you own it. It is yours. You would never say to your insurance company, "Yeah, give me the policy because I am going to total this thing today!"

Besides, they wouldn't give it to you if you said that! (We found out the hard way.)

This is the difference between renting and owning.

Renters are in this for a short time and don't think about the future too often, at least in this scenario.

On the other hand. . . . .

OWNERS ARE IN IT FOR THE LONG HAUL

PROBLEM SOLVERS

TRASH PICKER-UPPERS

BIGGER SPENDERS

And highly committed. (Remember signing those 1,054 mortgage papers at the house closing, or signing all of those documents when you bought your first car?)

Owners spend hours on weekends feverishly working on DIY projects to improve the value of their home. They buy mulch, flowers and fertilizer when they would rather buy a new laptop. Because they have a stake in the neighborhood, they show up at the HOA meetings even when they have a really busy week. They care about what affects the whole neighborhood, because this is their house.

Why do they do it?

Owners know they will invest more not less along the way, but get a bigger return on their investment. The day they sell their property, all of their hard work, sacrifice and time will pay off. They end up getting more back in the end.

The same principle applies when you volunteer:

As a renter, you're planning to give the minimal amount of you... enough to check off the "giving back" box, but not enough to build great memories, make great friendships or get your heart wrecked as you care about someone else.

If you just show up occasionally, you don't get to know anyone's story or see their life changed over time.

IF YOU SHOW UP THREE TIMES A YEAR, YOU WON'T IMPACT A CHILD'S FUTURE MUCH.

IF YOU SHOW UP ONCE A MONTH, IT WILL BE HARD TO BUILD SIGNIFICANT RELATIONSHIPS WITH KIDS OR TEENAGERS.

IF YOU SHOW UP ONLY DURING THE HOLIDAYS, YOU WILL MISS THE JOY THAT HAPPENS ALL YEAR LONG AND ONLY EXPERIENCE IT FOR A SEASON.

If you just stick your big toe in the water when it comes to helping someone else, you'll get one big toe's worth of life change.

Don't you want more than that? You're missing the best part! It's time to do something bigger, to invest more not less and get a bigger return on your investment.

Renting is normal. Owning isn't. Well, okay, owning is normal for some people, but owning with a paid-off house, a clean lawn, and an impeccable record with the neighborhood isn't.

If you want to be a not normal volunteer, you need to be an owner, not a renter.

OWNERS BELIEVE DEEPLY IN WHAT THEY ARE DOING

Let's start with a question that hopefully hits you right between the eyes: "Do you believe in the cause that you

IF YOU WANT TO BE A NOT
NORMAL VOLUNTEER, **YOU
NEED TO BE AN OWNER,
NOT A RENTER.**

are volunteering for?" If you don't and you are just doing it because someone coaxed you into it or you are just checking a box, you are definitely going to wind up a renter and not an owner.

Owners are convinced that what they are doing is important. There is a compelling reason behind their volunteering. For them, it's personal.

NO ONE SHOULD HAVE TO EAT OUT OF A GARBAGE CAN.

EVERY VILLAGE SHOULD HAVE CLEAN WATER.

EVERY KID NEEDS A PLACE TO BELONG.

NO SINGLE PARENT SHOULD FEEL ISOLATED.

EVERY TEENAGER NEEDS ANOTHER ADULT WHO BELIEVES IN THEM.

SENIORS DESERVE SOMEONE TO VISIT AND CARE FOR THEM.

NO DISASTER SHOULD LACK LIFE-SAVING MEDICAL ASSISTANCE.

If you believe in a cause, then your belief fuels your passion to care for others and you serve with an excellence that inspires those around you. Whenever you meet a volunteer owner, they make an unforgettable impression.

Volunteers who have an ownership approach are very easy to identify. They are the people who believe so deeply in what they are doing that they

EMBRACE VISION.

TALK ABOUT IT ON SOCIAL MEDIA.

DON'T MIND WEARING THE T-SHIRT THAT THEY ARE "ENCOURAGED" TO WEAR.

DO UNTHINKABLE THINGS FOR THE CAUSE THEY SO DEEPLY BELIEVE IN.

I (Sue) met one such volunteer in a hospital setting, during one of the scariest days of my life.

When I was diagnosed with an early stage of breast cancer, I needed surgery. The day it was scheduled, the hospital staff was competent, efficient and medically savvy. I, on the other hand, was quiet, anxious and scared.

While waiting for like a million years in pre-op, an engaging volunteer named Gwyn stopped in for a visit.

Gwyn wasn't normal – and I could sense it almost immediately.

She took the lead in the conversation, letting me know that six years ago she had been sitting in this same hospital walking through the first stages of breast cancer too.

As she talked, I was drawn to her. She understood how scary all of this was. My guard started to come down a little. She was now a survivor and believed I was going to be one too.

I started to let myself believe that just a little for the very first time.

The words on this page that you are reading really do not describe what I felt. All because of what Gwyn did in those first few moments.

She handed me a gift bag she had been holding and told me to open it. She was smiling ear-to-ear as she handed it to me, so excited that I was going to see what was inside.

I reached in past the white tissue paper overflowing out the top and yanked out the softest, furriest stuffed lion ever.

HANDMADE

JUST FOR ME

BY GWYN AND A TEAM OF OTHER SURVIVORS

Not only was the lion cute, but it had a purpose. It was going to help me keep my arm propped up in recovery position as I was healing.

The lion had a nametag tied to its neck. His name was COURAGE.

Whenever I felt afraid in the weeks ahead, the lion's nametag would serve as a reminder that I could win this fight with cancer. There was a team of women who thought so. They were cheering for me. I wasn't alone.

Gwyn's phone number was on the back of the nametag.

When I saw that phone number is when I totally lost it.

When someone loves for free, it's powerful. When someone gives you hope on your scariest day, it's unforgettable.

Gwyn believed deeply in what she was doing. She believed in it so deeply that she gave her time, for free, to see others receive hope, joy and peace during some scary, scary times.

Do you believe deeply in what you are doing?

Owners do.

9 THINGS A RENTER WON'T TELL YOU

1. **That dog barking uncontrollably down the hall is so cute and fluffy.** We can't wait until his owner goes out of town again and he barks for 24 hours straight. It is literally the highlight of our year!

2. **We love our stark white appliances!** They are coming back in style!

3. **The neighbors are really quiet.** Those large gatherings that they have must be their monthly Book Club meeting.

4. **The mail comes on time, the same time every day.** And the postman is so friendly!

5. **The leasing office/landord is so nice.** They are the friendliest, warmest, most gentle people you will ever meet. And they would NEVER raise our rent. We think these people should be featured on Oprah's next special they are so nice.

6. **We are so happy that we can't have a grill on our balcony.** We don't miss the mouth-watering flavor of grilled chicken, steaks or fish anyway. Who likes that?

7. **My wife just took a decorating class and is going to make this house her first project.**

8. **Our carpet is new and fresh.** There are no stains. They really put some dollars into making this "top-notch" for us!

9. **We love renting.** It is fulfilling all of our hopes and dreams.

OWNERS PUSH THE LIMITS

There are times when what used to work isn't working anymore.

THESE NINE-YEAR-OLD BOYS WANT TO RUN AROUND ON SUNDAY MORNING, AND NOT MEMORIZE THEIR VERSE.

THIS SPECIAL NEEDS PRETEEN NEEDS A FRIEND, NOT JUST A PROGRAM.

THIS ELDERLY PERSON NEEDS A COMPUTER, NOT JUST A MEAL ON WHEELS.

THIS SINGLE MOM NEEDS A JOB, NOT JUST COATS TO KEEP HER KIDS WARM.

A normal way of thinking would be to just let these things stay the way they are because that's the way they have always been even though they might not still work.

Owners push the limits to work on solutions. They go over and above what is expected to push for what is really needed instead.

Like Joel, who took his small group of nine-year-old boys to the gym and let them run relays while they memorized their verse.

Like Kristi, a middle school small group leader who pushed the envelope when she added the special needs preteen to her small group of girls. Turns out it was a good thing for everyone involved. The special needs student received love and encouragement from a group of friends every Tuesday night, something she had never had before. The middle school girls got their hearts stretched and grown as they showed love to someone whose life was very different than theirs.

Like Doug, an IT guy who collected money from a bunch of other IT analysts at work and brought a very surprised elderly person a brand new computer. Turns out that he needed one to communicate with his grandkids.

Joel, Kristi and Doug aren't normal.

Owners don't see problems. They see opportunities for new solutions.

Owners understand that what has worked for a long time, maybe even for generations, needs to be adapted and modified to help a current generation grow in a different way than a previous one did.

It comes from their deep belief that what they're doing matters more than how they're doing it, so they are determined to serve whoever is on the other end of the need. Whatever it takes.

Now, don't get us wrong here. Owners also know and understand that this "Pushing the Limits" thing also has boundaries. They understand that they can't come in and push crazy ideas that are not in line with the overall vision. They have enough respect for their leader that they operate within the context of their cause.

This is a tricky thing that makes an owner so valuable.

Time after time we have seen volunteers come into programs, particularly in churches, and suggest ideas that don't align with their leader's vision. Then, when the leader has to turn them down, the volunteers quit because they didn't get their own way. That is like a renter breaking his or her lease because they couldn't knock down a wall between the spare bedroom and living room.

Owners know better.

We will talk about this in much more detail in Chapter 5, "Honor the Leader."

Owners push the limits to resolve conflict. They are convinced that the mission that we're all doing together is more important than any one person's agenda, or hurt feelings.

When tension rises as passionate people bump heads over decisions that need to be made, owners commit to getting the right people around the table, and working things out.

UNDERSTANDING PREVAILS.

GRACE PREVAILS.

GENTLENESS WITH HOW WE TREAT EACH OTHER PREVAILS.

After all, we can't really love and help others without loving each other first and that means working through the tough stuff.

We heard a story recently about some conflict that happened on a vocal team in a kids program at a church.

First off, let's just state this: if you volunteer in any capacity on the stage, you are special. We can say this because we both have volunteered and work on stage, and we know we are special. Not always a good sort of "special". After all, we have special personalities that make us gifted for such a task. It is also difficult for us to keep our egos in check. To be owners, we have to understand the bigger picture: it isn't about us.

Back to the story. There was a seasoned vocalist. She was in her early 40s and there was a rumor that she was being replaced by a younger college-aged male vocalist. The rumor was not true, but she didn't know that at the time. Her feelings got hurt. She had dedicated a lot of time to this particular program and she felt she was being pushed out the door.

The person believed to be executing this decision was the leader of the vocal team, who was also a volunteer.

The woman approached the leader of the team in a calm way. She didn't do it with anger or resentment. She did it hoping to end up with a solution to resolve how she was feeling internally. These two leaders sat down, hashed it out and discussed the rumors and false-truths that were being shared. In the end, they arrived at a peaceful understanding.

They are both owners. Had they been renters they might have started gossiping behind each other's backs, dragged other folks into the situation, and created a whirlwind of controversy over an issue that really wasn't an issue at all.

If they were normal, this would have turned out a lot differently.

Owners push the limits to innovate. These are the folks who are trying to do what they do in new and creative ways to help a leader accomplish the vision he or she has set forth.

Consistently innovating and dreaming up different ideas and new things singlehandedly helps us stay ahead of the curve.

Whether that is coming up with new ways to

TAKE ATTENDANCE

MAKE YOUR ENVIRONMENT MORE APPEALING

TELL A BIBLE STORY

COMMUNICATE WITH TEENAGERS

PARTNER WITH PARENTS

Volunteers who are owners are always suggesting, presenting, and collaborating on new ideas to help things work better. We want you to be one of those.

OWNERS INVEST MORE FOR A BIGGER RETURN

When you buy a house, you are expecting to make money. Well, maybe not so much anymore, but this used to hold absolutely true. You had to put in quite a bit more money up front, usually a down payment, but at the end of the day, you ended up selling with a bigger return.

If that has happened to you, doesn't it feel great? You invested wisely on the front end, worked hard to take care of it along the way, and then years later, you get a bigger return back than what you put in originally. What a feeling!

The same is true about people who have an ownership mentality about volunteering. They invest more up front for a larger return in the end.

Owners could easily make a list of things they are giving as they volunteer.

TWO HOURS A WEEK

MONEY

EXPERTISE

PHYSICAL LABOR

EMOTIONAL ENERGY

But, most owners will never talk to you about what they had to give up each week.

They are much more focused on how rich their lives feel and how much they are gaining while they are serving. They don't get sucked into the controversy that surrounds programs or departments when difficult decisions need to be made. They focus on giving back rather than the problems that could distract them.

Owners understand, and even like, that they have to. . . . .

ARRIVE AT EVENTS SUPER-EARLY

HELP SET UP FOOD FOR OTHER VOLUNTEERS

SWEEP UP POPCORN AFTER EVENTS ARE OVER

GO TO ALL-NIGHT LOCK-INS WITH TEENAGERS

And they don't want anything in return for it.

In the beginning of this chapter I (Sue) mentioned a woman named Gwyn. Well, there is a little more to this story.

I went to visit Gwyn and her team of volunteers to say thank you after my surgery. I thought I might see a group of women intently huddled over their sewing projects. After all, what they were doing was so important.

Instead, I walked into a group of women animatedly telling stories about who they had given lions to last week. There was laughter and joy and there were even some tears around that table. They were energized, eyes shining brightly as they spoke…fully alive.

I told them how much I appreciated them, and how grateful I was to have been on the receiving end of their work. I asked them how long they had been together.

They had been making these lions for more than six years.

Why did they do it every week? Here are a few of the things they said:

THEY WERE DOING SOMETHING SIGNIFICANT.

IT GAVE THEM PURPOSE.

FULFILLMENT WAS OFF THE CHARTS.

THEY FELT LOVED WHEN THEY WERE SICK AND WANTED TO GIVE SOME LOVE BACK.

THERE WAS A SENSE OF ADVENTURE.

THEY KNEW WHAT IT WAS LIKE TO FIGHT CANCER.

It's ironic that you start out as a volunteer worried about the time you may be losing in your busy schedule. Renting seems like a great option, because that way you won't lose too much. Your investment is small. But so is your return.

Quirky owners pray harder, work harder and give more. They push to make a bigger investment in someone else's life. The more they do it, the more convinced they become over time. It's wisest to invest bigger in someone else's life, because there's simply so much for you to gain.

Owners aren't normal.

IT'S WISEST TO INVEST
BIGGER IN SOMEONE
ELSE'S LIFE, BECAUSE
**THERE'S SIMPLY SO MUCH
FOR YOU TO GAIN.**

1

CARPET STEAM CLEANER

Is this the most complicated thing that man has ever created? The water goes here, the cleaning solution goes there, and I couldn't even find a place for the bleach that was recommended for difficult areas. Funniest thing was, as soon as I fired this thing up for the first time, it blew three circuits in my house! I had to call an electrician!

BIKES

Renting a bike is one of my absolute most favorite things to do on vacation. My extended family of 15 spends a week together in Hilton Head every summer, and we all ride bikes together in the evenings. We race, we ride through shallow tide pools on the beach, and are always on the lookout for alligators along the way.

2

DOG-CLIPPING SHEARS

This was a one-time rental for me. When you get a new puppy, most people think, "Sure, I could cut this dog's hair." After I was done with my first professional clipping, my poor dog was butchered. He looked like he could win one of those ugly-dog competitions that used to air on the USA Network before PETA got involved. Poor baby. I took him to a groomer the next time.

3

SUE HAS RENTED

CONFETTI CANNONS

4

I love to create moments in ministry where kids and families go "Wow! I have never seen that before!" That is one of the reasons I loved renting confetti cannons. To see those beauties go off and fly little pieces of paper throughout a room brought me so much joy! The only people that it didn't bring joy to was the janitorial staff. They cursed me.

POST-HOLE DIGGER

My husband and I decided to put up a fence at our house when we lived in the Midwest. All I can say is: Digging post-holes is a whole lot of work! I was exhausted after we were finished! The next time we needed one, we rented an automatic one. Much easier.

5

ADAM HAS RENTED

HELIUM TANK

If you're like me and have been in ministry awhile, you have probably rented a helium tank at least once. Helium tanks are the best! Mainly because when you are around one, everyone begins to act like they are in fourth grade again. The wheels come off the cart pretty quick! The last time I rented a helium tank, I ended up with a funny new voicemail for callers to enjoy.

NISSAN CUBE

Have you seen this car? I thought it looked kind of cool and decided to rent one on a trip. I could not have made a worse decision. The car was clunky to drive, difficult to steer, and had the worst blind spot I have ever seen (or not seen). Memorable, but for the wrong reasons!

A PADDLEBOARD

3

Where I live on Fort Lauderdale Beach, paddleboard rental stations are set up along the sand. It is pretty difficult to stand up on this board, and if the water is choppy, forget about it. I generally panic as I get about a hundred feet out, as the possibility of encountering a shark races through my mind. It is then I turn back and kindly return the rental.

A CHAINSAW

4

We recently did some renovation work in our offices and we didn't have a church chainsaw. So I went to a hardware store to rent one. First, the clerk took one look at me and said, "You're renting a chainsaw?" I replied, "Do I not look like I can manage a chainsaw?" She said, "You're wearing flip flops." I rented the chainsaw anyway and sure enough, ended up with a foot injury. She was right.

COLLEGE TEXTBOOKS

5

Did you know that this was even an option? I didn't either until someone tipped me off to it. I saved so much money in college by doing this!

CHA

PTER

4

YOU, ME, WE

Quirk four: **This is not about me. It's not about you. It's about how WE do this together.**

We've noticed that not normal volunteers work together differently than most.

It has to do with putting aside personal agendas and deciding to work on one bigger agenda that drew everyone together in the first place.

They know that something out of the ordinary happens whenever you get a group of people together who all have something in common. Something not at all normal.

There's a sense of camaraderie that emerges whenever....

YOU SIT IN THE STANDS WATCHING YOUR SPORTS TEAM PLAY

YOU JOIN A CLUB

A DISASTER HAPPENS IN YOUR TOWN

YOU ATTEND A SUPPORT GROUP

YOU ARE THE PARENT OF A TEENAGER

YOUR FLIGHT GETS GROUNDED FOR 24 HOURS DUE TO A SNOWSTORM

Whenever you find yourself with people who are experiencing the same thing you are, connection happens. No matter who you talk to, no matter if things are funny, sad, frustrating or fantastic, you can identify with each other. You're all in the same boat. You are all sharing the same moment.

Like when your team has a winning season and goes on to win the big trophy. The entire town shares the moment. People tweet about it, talk about it, and replay the highlight videos on their phones. Banners and signs light up the downtown area as shop owners go over the top to show their support. Strangers will high-five anyone else wearing a team jersey as if they made the winning play themselves. The people in the town feel like they've all won something because they identify with this team. This is their team.

What started out as a normal "you" and "me" situation quickly turned into a not normal collective "we" experience. Some collective experiences last for an hour or two, some a couple of months or years, but others can last a lifetime.

When I (Sue) was in my twenties, I became part of a merry band of young, inexperienced college students fired up about starting a church in the northwest suburbs of Chicago. We wanted a place to bring our friends who didn't attend church. We talked together about a local church where the music would be done with excellence, the creative arts would be embraced and the messages would be relevant and engaging. We imagined a church where relationships were real and honest like the community we read about in the early church in Acts. 2. We had never been to a church like that, but we wanted a church like that for our friends and family members who didn't know God. We wanted that with every ounce of passion we had within us.

Now we had no money and no experience. But fortunately, we also didn't have enough wisdom to let that stop us. As a small, optimistic volunteer core, we scraped together every last cent we had, sold whatever we could, and rented a movie theater in Palatine, Illinois. My parents thought we were crazy, in way over our heads. They thought we were flying by the seat of our pants. They were actually right on both accounts. Normal people would have halted plans right then and there. But we held our very first church service on Sunday, October 12, 1975.

To say this challenge was hard would be an understatement. The hours were forever long.

We did everything ourselves…

CLEANUP

REHEARSALS

PLANNING MEETINGS

CARE VISITS

COMMUNITY GROUPS

HIGH SCHOOL MINISTRY

CHILDREN'S MINISTRY

WHATEVER WAS NEEDED

We worked our regular daytime jobs to pay our bills, and volunteered our free time to help where we could. The financial pressure was intense. We were always a week away from financial disaster in those first couple of years.

But we weren't giving up.

Much to our surprise, God used our efforts and brought in all kinds of people Sunday after Sunday.

The church started to grow.

As a schoolteacher, I invited two teachers I hung out with to come with me. I watched them start to open the door to what a real relationship with God might look like in their own lives. We began to have great conversations about it at school. I could hardly contain myself! This was huge. It made this mission personal for me. They were the reason we did all of this. And moments like theirs were happening to others all around me as well.

We saw lives changed, marriages turned around, families put back together again, and community built in smaller groups. Our core group watched in absolute wonder as we saw prayer after prayer answered in supernatural ways. We lived with a keen awareness that we were on a God-sized adventure of a lifetime.

But the most joyful discovery for me was the deep friendships that were built with those pioneers. We started out as individuals passionate about the same dream. But, somehow, over time, that changed to a not at all normal "we."

We did real life with each other.

My best friend Lynne and I would often escape to Dairy Queen when we were overwhelmed by the pace. Both of our husbands were neck-deep in this start up, and as young couples we struggled to keep some kind of balance in our marriages. Over hot fudge sundaes, we would listen and problem-solve with each other. We discovered that it makes all the difference in the world to have someone else breathe life back into you after a really draining week.

WE STARTED OUT AS INDIVIDUALS PASSIONATE ABOUT THE SAME DREAM. BUT, **SOMEHOW, OVER TIME, THAT CHANGED TO A NOT AT ALL NORMAL "WE."**

Sometimes after an especially long night of set-up or rehearsals, a group of us would go out to the same cheap restaurant, starving and exhausted. Over burgers and fries we would start reconnecting about our personal lives, and what was really going on inside of us. Eventually we would start telling stories that made us laugh so hard that our stomachs hurt. We left ready to do it all over again the next time. Those were the moments that kept us alive so we could make it through another week.

One night, we discovered how important it is to encourage each other. We had gathered for a strategy meeting about the future. To close our time together, our leader asked us to write words of encouragement on each person's poster board around the circle. At the bottom, if we wanted to, we could give each other what he called "a blank check commitment" with our names signed at the bottom. It was our way of letting that person know we were going to be there – no matter how that check got filled in during the year ahead. It was a powerful time as we gifted each other with written words.

At home that night, I got emotional as I read through the names of those who had given me a blank check commitment. How do you even respond to someone that generous to you? How do you process that kind of friendship? There just are no words to describe love like that.

But I also eagerly read the notes that had been written to me personally. Some were hilarious. Others told me how I had specifically impacted their life over the past year. Those meant the world to me. Then there were those that contained the shocker word of all time for me.

"Leader."

These friends saw leadership in me. They thought I was a leader. What?

No one had ever told me I could lead something in my entire life. This was all new to me. I thought, wow, that's a nice thing to know. Then I filed it away and promptly forgot about it.

Until years later, when I was living in Tennesee with my husband and two children, Holly and Ryan.

I got a phone call from Don, the associate pastor at Willow Creek Community Church, asking me to consider leading their children's ministry. After I picked myself up off the floor, I kindly said I didn't think so, I really didn't have any experience, but I would pray about it (like for about ten years maybe!).

One week later, I got a call from the senior pastor, Bill Hybels, asking me to pray faster and just say yes. He told me that he wanted me to come and build a national caliber children's ministry for the sake of the kids and their parents who didn't attend any local church in that area.

The possibility and sound of this made my heart start to pound and beat faster. I had experienced this feeling before . . . years ago in a movie theater with this same band of merry leaders.

A few weeks later, I said yes and moved back to the northwest suburbs of Chicago with my family to work at Willow Creek Community Church. For seventeen years, I worked alongside hundreds of not normal volunteers who wanted to build faith in the next generation. I had the time of my life all over again.

Only when I take the time to look back through my story do I see how clearly my friends helped set me up to win. Their words, written to me on my poster board, were used to steer my path toward the role I was going to play in the future.

What's amazing to me now is that forty years later, most of those friendships are still intact. To be sure, our situations have changed dramatically. We aren't all living in Chicago. We aren't all serving at Willow Creek Community Church. We aren't twenty anymore. We don't see each other as much as we did then. But whenever our paths do cross, we look each other in the eye and still feel that not normal deep connection. We know what we shared together. We remember what we saw God do together. We know that He used us to do something bigger together than any one of us could have ever done alone.

Those days in my twenties shaped how I view volunteers and value their worth. I want every volunteer to be led the way Bill led me. I want every not normal volunteer to experience serving the quirky way I did, living out their faith while pursuing a Kingdom adventure in this world that sets their soul on fire. Nothing compares to that "WE" kind of serving…..absolutely nothing.

So, let's look at how you can experience that for yourself. It's simpler than you think.

"WE" LIKE TO BE KNOWN

Have you ever walked into a volunteer situation where no one really knows each other? Doesn't that feel weird and awkward? Yikes. No one is connected relationally because each person is only focused on the task or person in front of them. The environment feels stiff, way too quiet, emotionally distant. Even though people are courteous to one another, it is in the most superficial way. It's no surprise that at the end of the hour, people scurry to get their coats on as if they can't get out the door fast enough. That's what normal feels like.

Contrast that picture with one where everyone in the room knows each other. These people draw you into their circle when you first arrive. They introduce themselves and warmly welcome you to their team.

It's clear these volunteers....

KNOW EACH OTHER'S NAMES

LAUGH AND JOKE AROUND

FEEL HAPPY TO BE THERE

ASK ABOUT EACH OTHER'S FAMILY

ENCOURAGE EACH OTHER

CARE ABOUT THE KIND OF WEEK EACH ONE HAD

This is what not normal feels like. Which picture is more appealing?

Which group of volunteers do you think have a more enjoyable time together while serving?

Exactly.

See, "We" like to be known. No one likes to feel isolated or alone. So, are you wondering how they got to know each other while busy with the role they were there to accomplish?

Good question.

They spent some time intentionally each week getting to know and care about each other before or after they served together. They made a commitment to show up and get connected with one another, believing in the end result.

We came up with a way to help our volunteers connect with each other before they went off to their separate areas each week. We invite all of them to circle up with a coach and get to know each other. We give them a chance to look side to side at who they are serving next to.

We call that time together a "huddle." It makes this concept practical, and when done consistently over time, has proven to be a great relationship-builder.

Huddle might be a really great name or a really cheesy name but that is what we called it. During these times, our coaches will cast vision reminding everyone why what they are there to do is significant, then give all those around the circle a chance to tell about the best thing that happened to them this week. Then, each one shares how these friends could best pray for them during the week. We aim for 15 minutes together before all of us start to serve. This has proved to be life-changing for our volunteers, because they listen and care about each other before they start caring about the ones they are there to serve.

There is a coach at a startup church that was at the very beginning of creating a not normal volunteer environment. She noticed that there was very little interaction with the seven volunteers in her ministry. They had no relationship with each other, so that sense of everybody working together towards the same goal was absent. They were missing the "We" factor.

So she thought she would try to help them get to know each other.

She knew that she couldn't force relationship, but she did think that she could help facilitate possible relationships and make her team stronger.

One day this coach circled up her small group leaders and led a very simple prayer before they went in to be with their small groups for the day. Before she released them, because they were literally in a circle, she said something that challenged them. She told them, "I want you to look side to side. There is a person on each side of you, and more than likely you don't know anything about these people. This month I want you to take some time and get to know the person standing on each side of you. I think that will help us become a stronger team."

Even though it always seemed like a hassle to carve out the extra 15 minutes on the front end of the commitment, they always ended up seeing the benefit on the backside.

They huddled up with each other and got to know. . . . .

WHICH STUDENT NEEDED A COLLEGE REFERENCE

WHO JUST LOST THEIR JOB

WHO JUST GOT A BAD MEDICAL REPORT

WHO WAS HAVING A NEW BABY

WHO SOLD THEIR HOUSE

WHICH TEENAGER WAS STRUGGLING

WHICH PRAYER JUST GOT ANSWERED

WHO GOT ENGAGED OVER THE WEEKEND

WHOSE FAMILY WAS COMING APART

They prayed with and for each other. They cheered the really good things, and encouraged whoever was struggling. Each one felt valued and supported by the team of people they served alongside. That helped give them what they needed most so they could serve someone else better.

They moved from the normal me and you serving experience to the not normal WE experience. It made all the difference in the world.

Here's the really awesome part.

One never knows what may happen as a result of that connected huddle time.

THAT HIGH SCHOOL STUDENT GOT A GREAT COLLEGE REFERENCE.

TWO VOLUNTEERS OUT OF JOBS PUT THEIR HEADS TOGETHER AND STARTED A SUCCESSFUL BUSINESS.

ONE SINGLE MOM MET HER FUTURE HUSBAND.

THE FAMILY THAT HAD A DAUGHTER WITH A BRAIN TUMOR RECEIVED MEALS AND A CLEAN HOUSE BECAUSE OF THAT CIRCLE. THOSE VOLUNTEERS PRAYED UP A STORM FOR HEALING!

CUPCAKES WERE BROUGHT IN TO CELEBRATE THE "SHE SAID YES" MOMENT.

Huddle becomes a quirky place where we get to know each other, around a table, or chairs, or a circle of beanbags sitting on the floor.

If we give a little extra time in order to be known and connected, it could establish a sense of community in each of our lives.

As volunteers get to know each other, the whole serving environment in their space becomes more engaging. There is a warmth and energy that permeates their room that comes when friends are familiar with each other. It becomes an appealing place for you to serve and for others to join, because the friendships are the real deal.

Here's how you can get quirkier:

START GETTING TO KNOW THE PEOPLE YOU SERVE ALONGSIDE.

IF WE GIVE A LITTLE
EXTRA TIME IN ORDER
TO BE KNOWN AND
CONNECTED, **IT COULD
ESTABLISH A SENSE OF
COMMUNITY IN EACH OF
OUR LIVES.**

COMMIT TO REGULARLY SHARING WHAT'S GOING ON IN YOUR OWN LIFE.

GIVE A LITTLE EXTRA OF YOUR TIME BELIEVING IT IS GOING TO BE WORTH IT.

Look side to side once in awhile and take the first step that leads you and me to becoming the not normal "We."

"WE" LIKE TO DO THINGS TOGETHER

When facing any huge challenge, its always more fun to do things with others rather than all by yourself.

Some people....

EXERCISE TOGETHER TO STAY MOTIVATED

TAKE TURNS SPRING-CLEANING EACH OTHER'S HOUSES

DO HOME PROJECTS WITH NEIGHBORS

CLEAN MOTORCYCLES WITH FRIENDS

BAKE DOZENS OF CHRISTMAS COOKIES TOGETHER

LANDSCAPE EACH OTHER'S YARDS

Work is just easier to get done when the load is shared with other people. It's more motivating and enjoyable to work together with other people who are passionate about the same thing you are. And you get better results too.

We think people like to party.

A party is a representation of people having fun working together.

This is why people...

SPEND THOUSANDS OF DOLLARS TO GO ON VACATION

GO TO THEIR HIGH SCHOOL REUNIONS

CELEBRATE THE HOLIDAYS WITH THEIR CO-WORKERS IN GRAND FASHION

ENJOY WEDDING RECEPTIONS

Because they want to party.

Parties can wear a lot of different faces (we personally like the big nose with the Groucho glasses), but having fun is common to all of them. Some people don't like big parties. They prefer smaller gatherings instead. No matter the size, though, people enjoy a good time with their friends. It's the people that make it a party.

Both of us have had some of the most fun we have had in our entire lives with the people that we have volunteered with. Not only did we have fun serving alongside them, but we have made some of the best, lifelong friends that we have ever had. We would have never made these connections had we not taken some of these fun principles seriously.

The thing to keep in mind is that a choice needs to be made by every member to work together in team, to join the party, to have fun doing this thing together.

It is about looking side to side to see what is going on around you rather than just focusing on yourself.

WHEN YOU LOOK SIDE TO SIDE YOU ARE MADE AWARE OF NEEDS THAT NEED TO BE MET.

WHEN YOU LOOK SIDE TO SIDE YOU MAKE FRIENDS, SOME LIFELONG.

WHEN YOU LOOK SIDE TO SIDE YOU LEARN FROM OTHERS.

WHEN YOU LOOK SIDE TO SIDE YOU BUILD MEMORIES TOGETHER.

IT IS ABOUT LOOKING SIDE TO SIDE TO SEE **WHAT IS GOING ON AROUND YOU** RATHER THAN JUST FOCUSING ON YOURSELF.

It takes a bunch of not normal volunteers willing to combine their different skills and choose to work in tandem with each other rather apart.

We know this is easier said than done.

It requires a quirky commitment to move from caring more about what I am doing, or what you are doing, to caring most about what "we" are doing together. When that happens, then great teamwork can become a reality. That's when your team can swing for the fences and go after the really big hairy audacious goals.

Think back to a time when you were on a great team. Remember what it was like? Can you think of anything NOT to like about being on a great team? Even if you didn't win any state trophies, didn't you have a blast along the way?

Us too.

So let's think about what makes a team great.

Great teams enjoy unity because everyone is working toward the same goal. There is a mission, a cause that each individual signed up for. Every team member is clear about what they are on the team to do. Each one knows what success looks like, so everyone can celebrate whenever it happens. Every volunteer knows the compelling reason behind their work.

When the mission is clear, normal individual agendas about what the mission could be or should be can disappear because that's already been decided. No one needs to waste valuable time on that. Now that we all see what the mission is, how the mission gets accomplished can be open for discussion and new ideas. We choose to work together for that common good, laying aside our own personal agendas. That's how you start.

Great teams also appreciate each other's different skills. They realize a wide variety of abilities working together are needed to accomplish the goal. Every skill is valued and important. The truth is, we need lots of different abilities in order to make the biggest difference so everyone is welcome. . . . . .

ORGANIZERS

CREATIVES

PEOPLE DEVELOPERS

CAREGIVERS

COMMUNICATORS

MARKETERS

RECRUITERS

FINANCIAL EXPERTS

CHEFS

MUSICIANS

ARTISTS

SPECIAL NEEDS SPECIALISTS

Ask yourself, wherever you serve, is there anyone listed above that you couldn't put to good use? Wouldn't it be great to have all of these people with their different points of view working on your team? Can you imagine what you could accomplish? Wow. We need each other. Every person has a unique and significant contribution to make. We can learn from each other. We accomplish more and have greater impact when we work together.

Take the next step, get quirkier, and look at your own team.

IS EVERYONE THERE FOR THE SAME MISSION?

DO VOLUNTEERS FEEL LIKE THEIR UNIQUE SKILLS MATTER?

ANY IMPROVEMENTS THAT NEED TO BE MADE TO WORK BETTER TOGETHER?

Your team can be a great team. You might be just a tweak away from that, but this is totally within your reach.

And if it all works you've got one big quirky party on your hands.

"WE" LIKE TO GIVE OUR BEST

Normally, we don't really drift into doing our best at anything. Instead, we always need a reason to rise to the occasion.

We need a little push, don't we?

In school, our favorite teacher often turns out to be the one who makes us work the hardest because she won't settle for less than our best.

In sports, the irreplaceable coaches are the ones who believe in your potential and push you to get there.

At work, the most memorable bosses are those who sit across the table and ask you where you want to go in the company because they want to help you do your best to get there.

With friends, the best ones keep nudging you to take the next step toward becoming healthier or debt-free or more patient as a parent.

The same is true for not normal volunteers. You like when a leader encourages you to give your best effort. At Orange, we believe in excellence because we know it inspires others to do their best as well. (Reggie Joiner calls it "maximizing," which means we're never happy until we're all happy.) Excellence matters.

GOOD MUSICIANS INSPIRE AND ATTRACT OTHER GOOD MUSICIANS.

GOOD COMMUNICATORS INSPIRE OTHER GOOD COMMUNICATORS TO JOIN.

GOOD SMALL GROUP LEADERS INSPIRE OTHERS TO DO THE SAME IN THEIR GROUP.

Excellence is contagious.

Others want to be a part of something great that is done with excellence. High quality draws them in. It brings out the not normal inside of them as everyone remembers who it is we are doing all of this for in the first place. We want to honor God by giving Him our best.

Let's face it....

NO ONE LIKES SERVING IN A CHAOTIC ENVIRONMENT.

NO ONE ENJOYS POOR SINGING.

NO ONE LOOKS FORWARD TO THINGS BEING THROWN TOGETHER.

NO ONE FEELS GREAT ABOUT POOR CRAFTSMANSHIP.

NO ONE RAVES ABOUT RUDE ATTITUDES.

These environments don't inspire anyone to do their best. They promote a downward spiral toward greater apathy and mediocrity that gives whoever or whatever a bad name in our culture.

This is not a place where not normal volunteers hang out. No way do they stay here.

Not normal volunteers want to give their best. They like doing whatever they are doing with class. That is one of the quality quirky things we admire so much about them: They show up prepared and ready to go. They come ready to play hard, with a work ethic that just can't be beat. They inspire us and everyone around them over and over again. And they make Heaven smile at their efforts.

Now it's your turn. You can do this, you can be part of a not normal team too. Your quirkiness just needs to grow a little.

Start by realizing that this isn't about what you want.

IT'S NOT ABOUT WHAT I WANT.

IT'S ABOUT SOMETHING MUCH BIGGER THAN THAT.

IT'S ABOUT THE REALLY BIG SOMETHING THAT WE WANT TO MAKE HAPPEN TOGETHER.

"DENNIS AND SOME SOCKS"

Dennis was in his last year of high school. This had been a rough year on his faith because of things happening at home. In January, his not normal small group leader Kelly invited Dennis and the other guys in his group to give up a Friday night to serve the homeless together in a soup kitchen downtown. He thought it might be a good thing for them to experience before they graduated in spring.

Dennis loved making homemade spaghetti. He had learned how from his mom. He brought all of the ingredients with him the night his small group went so he could make it at the soup kitchen. His friends really got into it too, working hard to get everything done in time for dinner. Doors were opened at 5:30 and the regulars started streaming in. They couldn't get enough of the spaghetti. They raved about the sauce, and the meatballs were incredible! Most wanted seconds and thirds, eating until the huge pots were empty.

Dennis and his friends sat down with them and stayed for hours listening to a few of them tell their stories.

One week later, Dennis circled up his friends at school and made a bold request. He felt strongly that it was time to do something to help the people at the shelter. Turns out that several of them had mentioned their need for warm socks at their table that night. People never think to donate socks, so their feet were cold and wet all winter long, making their lives even more miserable. Their need struck a chord in Dennis and he couldn't let it go.

He recruited some help to pull off what he had in mind. He asked some students to create posters and put them all over school. He brainstormed with others how they could approach the teachers to ask for five minutes of class time on one certain day. He rallied good communicators who would be able to get students on board.

Student after student said yes and joined his team. They were inspired by his passion about this. He was determined to help his friends downtown. Excitement started to build, everyone anticipating what kind of response they would get from the students at large.

On Sock Day, the plan moved to implementation. Throughout the day, every hour began with a student making a five-minute pitch to a class about the homeless people who needed warm socks. It was cold even in the school, so students could easily relate. Students were asked to take their socks off right then and there and give them to someone who really needed them. And they did. Thousands of socks were collected in big black garbage bags, and went home with volunteers to get washed. That day, when that suburban high school let out, thousands of teenagers went home on buses with cold, wet feet for a really good cause. That's when the word started to spread like wild fire.

Somehow the news about what these high school kids had done made it to the local news that night and more people found out about the need for winter socks. Socks came flooding in from all directions, people inspired and wanting to get in on the action too.

A week later, thousands of homeless people received a gift at the shelter. They were able to pick from the socks all spread out on the tables there. They stared in amazement as they put their only pair of thick, warm socks on their feet. Where did these socks come from?

They would probably never believe it, but these socks were made possible by one anonymous not normal high school volunteer that pulled out the best in so many others.

1

OUR PONTOON BOAT

We live on Lake Lanier and have a party boat that can hold 10 people. Anytime we are out cruising with a warm breeze, gorgeous sunset, snacks and great friends, it's a party.

2

MY TWO GRANDSONS

Anytime I am hanging out with Levi and Landon, I am in party heaven. No one makes me laugh harder than those two!

5 THINGS
(ACCORDING TO SUE)
THAT MAKE
A QUIRKY PARTY

3

PORTILLO'S ITALIAN BEEF SANDWICHES

from Chicago. Since we live in Georgia, our family orders it and has it delivered on really special occasions. Chicago food is our jam.

4

WEST WING EPISODES

Love the pranks the staff members play on each other in the White House. I also have a little crush on President Bartlett as a leader. (This kind of makes for a nonpolitical *political* party, but a party's a party!)

5

FIREWORKS

in our driveway. I love the drama of watching my husband announce each one and then light them. The bangs and blasts always draw a crowd of happy people who love to watch the night sky light up with color and pop. We top it off with super-long sparklers to get everyone involved in the fun. This is great party experience for everyone (except for our dog who hates loud noises).

1 MY UNCLE DEREK

You don't know him, but he is hilarious. Add this man to any party and he is an instant hit. He comes to our Christmas party that Katelyn and I throw every year in Michigan and cracks the crowd up from start to finish. In 2012 he centered on the Mayan Calendar (because if you remember, the world was about the end) and he said to the crowd, "Everyone, if they're right we will save a few house payments!"

2 A TOAST

Regardless of what is in the glass, I love a party with a toast. Life is worth celebrating, and there is nothing better than recognizing that with an entire room of people toasting to it. If I have nothing to toast to, I generally toast to fallen President David Palmer from the television series 24. Why? Keeps people guessing...

3 MUSIC

Specifically a set of songs containing "Love Shack" by the B52s. No matter what age, this song gets the party going because everybody knows it. Just wait until the "Bang, Bang, Bang on the door baby" part. The entire room loses their minds!

5 THINGS

THAT MAKE
A QUIRKY PARTY

4

HIGH-TOP TABLES

These just seem to scream, "Stand around me and have a conversation!" I have had some of the best conversations in my life standing around a high-top table. They are a must for any party that is going to be considered a good one.

HOODY'S CAJUN SNACK MIX

5

If you have not heard of the best snack mix on the planet, you are seriously missing out. Not only is this stuff addictive, but if you are the one who brought this to the party, consider yourself the hit of the event! Not a ladies man? No problem. Come to the party with Hoody's Cajun Snack Mix and watch your life change.

CHA

PTER

5

HONOR THE LEADER

You'd be surprised how quirky it is to **trust, honor and follow the leader in charge of the area where you serve.**

All of us have an idea of what a church program should be like. And although our imaginations may take us to some interesting and intriguing places when it comes to those programs, the most important principle for a volunteer to remember is as old as a children's game: follow the leader.

What does that mean exactly?

First, let us be clear that there are some bad leaders who don't deserve to be followed. If you find yourself a follower of that kind of leader, you should move on and find something better to do with your valuable time. But most leaders are good, solid people who bring a vision forward and need people to help them execute it. Those are the not normal type of leaders we want to follow.

The two of us, Sue and Adam, are both leaders. Paid staff members. Not volunteers anymore.

We still volunteer for some things, but we've worked on church staffs and with non-profit organizations for many years.

This is an interesting topic for a chapter because your leaders are going to love that we wrote this, but you as the volunteer might struggle with it. Like we promised, quirky. That aside, we believe it is essential to going over and above as you volunteer. In fact, you will be going over and above in every area of your life if you get this.

Allow us to be blunt: **we need you.**

We need volunteers.

> **WE NEED YOU TO PRAY FOR US.**
>
> **WE NEED YOU TO LOVE US.**
>
> **WE NEED YOU TO SUPPORT US.**
>
> **WE NEED YOU TO HONOR AND EMBRACE THE VISION GOD HAS GIVEN US.**
>
> **AND SOMETIMES WE NEED YOU TO PROVIDE US PRESCRIPTION MEDICATION. (WE'RE KIDDING ABOUT THAT. RIGHT?)**

Your leaders feel a lot of pressure.

A lot.

They pour time and energy into this thing you are a part of. So cut them some slack. The decisions they make probably aren't random. So do your best to try to support them.

This can happen in big ways and little ways. We talked in the second chapter about how "Small is Big" and those principles of doing little things for big impact can apply to honoring your leader as well. They can range from as small

ALLOW US TO BE BLUNT:
WE NEED YOU.

as not complaining about the types of pencils that they picked out to as big as saying "Yes" to the vision they have for the church and local community. It could be as small as pretending you like the new carpet that was picked out to as big as standing next to your leader when someone else tries to take him or her down.

It is so important that volunteers stand next to their leader during good and difficult times. It makes a world of difference. That might be the most not normal thing that you can do as you serve. We know we say that a lot in this book – but that's because we really mean it.

Let's talk about some things you'll want to do, and some things you'll definitely not want to do, as you build an environment of honor around your leaders and leadership team.

EMBRACE THEIR VISION

That's one of the "you'll want to do" things. If you are a part of something where you don't embrace the vision, get out of it!

Your job as a volunteer is not to change the vision of a program that you are involved in. Your job is to support it, and hopefully that's what attracted you to the opportunity in the first place.

It will absolutely drain you to be a part of a vision you do not support.

YOU WILL WANT TO QUIT.

YOU WILL GO HOME EXHAUSTED.

YOU WILL THINK ABOUT WAYS TO CHANGE THIS TO BE SOMETHING YOU WANT IT TO BE.

YOUR JOB AS A VOLUNTEER IS NOT TO CHANGE THE VISION OF A PROGRAM THAT YOU ARE INVOLVED IN. YOUR JOB IS TO SUPPORT IT, AND HOPEFULLY THAT'S WHAT ATTRACTED YOU TO THE OPPORTUNITY IN THE FIRST PLACE. **IT WILL ABSOLUTELY DRAIN YOU TO BE A PART OF A VISION YOU DO NOT SUPPORT.**

When you support the vision a leadership group has set forth, it is like you are a part of a team. You are rallying around this vision with a cadre of people who believe in it too. It is so fun to be a part of.

In most cases, God gives vision and mission to leaders who are in charge. It is then the leader's responsibility to develop a strategy that goes alongside of that vision and mission. This is a very difficult thing for leaders to do. Most do not come to this lightly. It takes a long time to plan, articulate, and defend a vision.

Vision is a tricky thing when it comes to faith, because all of us have our own history of how we came to faith.

The truth is that you grew up and learned to practice your faith

IN A CERTAIN WAY

WITH CERTAIN LIGHTING

APPLYING SPECIFIC METHODS

ON CERTAIN CARPET SQUARES

WITH A DISTINCTIVE SMELL

RIDING IN A TYPE OF VAN THAT WENT OUT OF PRODUCTION IN 1992

WITH THINKING OR THINGS THAT MAY BE OUTDATED TODAY

It is good to celebrate the way that you came to know something, but you should never let that interfere with a leader who is being inspired to reach the next generation. God is working in his or her life to develop new methods of innovation and technique to accomplish that goal.

So let's say it again: If you can't support the vision that he or she has set forth, then it is time for you move on.

Let it go, as Elsa says.

Elsa isn't normal.

And Olaf surely isn't normal, but now we're getting off track.

We love helping volunteers find their right place.

That is a difficult statement because often that means we shift volunteers from one role to another, even from a role that they might enjoy doing to a role they may not see yet. Sometimes people are just in the wrong place.

We love the process of helping a person find where he or she truly fits in the grand scheme of things. A lot of times people are in the wrong spots simply because they can't embrace the vision of the program.

There is a girl I (Adam) know named Lisa. She is a sweet person. Lisa was one of our Worship Leaders in our Elementary Ministry department early on in her volunteering days. She was really talented and loved kids. The issue wasn't anything related to her commitment or her ability. The issue with her was related to the vision of what we wanted to be and what she wanted to be.

See, Lisa thought that worship was a show. Allow us to explain… (To preface, this might be the most un-normal example of us illustrating what it means to be normal and not "not normal." Confused? You won't be.)

Lisa loved to wear costumes when she was leading worship. On the front end there doesn't seem to be a problem with this, but when you dig deeper there is a huge problem.

We wanted worship for kids to be authentic. We wanted them to see real people expressing themselves to a real God in a real way. We wanted them to dress as they normally are and we wanted them to express themselves as they felt led to express themselves. Lisa didn't want to do this.

One Sunday, Lisa emerged from backstage in a full costume and didn't ask anyone if that might be a good idea. She had gone into the costume room when no one was looking and came out dressed in a hula skirt, and had Hawaiian leis on her head and around her neck. (You can't make this up folks, seriously.)

The way she looked was random, unrelated to anything we were taking about that morning. It was unrelated to anything that we had promoted to our families. For all our families knew, we were having a Hawaiian luau with our kids and Lisa was the hula-dancing star. The only thing we needed was a roasted pig.

This incident didn't sit well with the leadership team, so we called a meeting with Lisa. The leaders of this particular program addressed this issue with her. Lisa did not appreciate how the conversation went and said she would continue to volunteer, but she wanted to do things her way. Basically, if we didn't allow her to wear whatever grass skirt or clown hat she wanted, then she was going to quit. We had a problem.

LISA DIDN'T EMBRACE THE VISION.

SHE DIDN'T UNDERSTAND IT.

SHE THOUGHT HER WAY WAS BETTER.

AND SHE THREW A FIT WHEN SHE DIDN'T GET WHAT SHE WANTED.

LISA WAS VERY UN-NORMAL, BUT IN THE SAME BREATH, SHE WAS WAY TOO NORMAL.

We kindly asked her to step aside. She, in the meantime, got involved in a local community theatre and was much happier.

Maybe that is you.

MAYBE YOU ARE A PART OF SOMETHING THAT YOU THINK SHOULD BE DIFFERENT.

MAYBE YOU ARE A PART OF SOMETHING THAT YOU REALLY DON'T BELIEVE IN.

MAYBE YOU DON'T REALLY UNDERSTAND THE VISION OF WHAT YOU ARE A PART OF.

People often get confused on this topic. For some reason, over the course of time, people have looked at moving on as a bad thing or something negative. We think the opposite.

God has given you, as a volunteer, a perspective on how things should be done. We aren't telling you that you are wrong! But we are telling you that no matter how right you are, if your idea isn't in line with the current program you are involved in you need to be honest with yourself and your leaders. And any change that comes from these feelings should be considered a good one, even if it is hard.

Don't get this confused with "Push the Limits" that we talked about earlier. These are completely different. Pushing the limits is completely acceptable. Coming up with new ideas and helping your leader achieve vision in new and different ways is what we want you to do. But not embracing the vision of your leader is unacceptable.

Sometimes the best thing that a volunteer can do is amicably move on if they are in conflict with their leader over vision.

If that's you, make it happen.

BE A CHEERLEADER

So, that title might be a bit difficult for some of the male volunteers who are reading this book, but stay with us.

Cheerleaders are those on the sidelines of a game who are supporting their team. They cheer on their team no matter how good or how bad the team is doing. You never see the cheerleaders retreat into the locker room if the team is down by a few points. They are there through thick and thin.

I (Adam) was helping our church interview for a new position a few months ago and the lead candidate for the job was a former cheerleader for the Miami Dolphins football team. In case you were wondering, this was NOT the reason she got the position...she in fact was highly qualified for the marketing role we had in mind. But a question that I asked her about her former career stuck with me, and it is something that each individual volunteer can apply toward his or her ministry.

I asked her, "What is your favorite memory about your time with the Dolphins?"

She told me, "Whenever I cheered for them, it was a difficult time because we didn't win a whole lot of games. We had to look for something to get excited about. Instead of looking at the number of points on the scoreboard, we looked at the heart of the players. They had a ton of heart. Even though the points didn't rack up like we wanted them to."

Allow us to share some massive insight for a moment.

Here's something that your leader won't tell you, but we will. Leading people toward a cause is extremely difficult, time-consuming, and energy draining...especially in churches.

SOMETIMES THE BEST THING THAT A VOLUNTEER CAN DO IS AMICABLY MOVE ON IF THEY ARE IN CONFLICT WITH THEIR LEADER OVER VISION.

Sometimes it is borderline brutal.

You might not know this, but your leader has to deal with some pretty difficult things all in a week's time.

They have to deal with...

TRAGEDIES

DIVORCES

COMPLAINTS

BUDGETS

DISUNITY

WEEKEND PREP

AND VERY FEW COMPLIMENTS

I know what you are thinking: "I'm a volunteer and I work for free. Shouldn't I get what I want or be able to say what I want?" You might think so. But if you are in it with that attitude, you are already in it for the wrong reason. We would call that an "extremely normal" type of attitude, certainly not quirky or not normal.

If you're going to be a not normal kind of a volunteer you need to understand that your leader needs...

ENCOURAGEMENT

PATIENCE

WISDOM

KINDNESS

AND MORE...

Your leader needs a cheerleader.

Someone who is not normal is a cheerleader for his or her leaders at all times.

Let's reverse for a quick second. Sometimes a volunteer who is not normal has a legitimate concern or an issue. Being a cheerleader doesn't mean that you don't address that concern, but it does mean is that you address it in the right way with the right attitude.

We have heard so many stories about volunteers complicating staff members' lives when they

RESIGN BECAUSE THEY DON'T GET THEIR WAY

GOSSIP TO OTHER VOLUNTEERS ABOUT AN INCIDENT THAT WENT DOWN

DECIDE THAT THEY KNOW MORE THAN THE LEADER WHO IS HELPING TO CAST THE VISION

Jesus is pretty clear about how to resolve conflict with someone, and this includes other volunteers you interact with and your leaders.

You've likely read the passage from Matthew 18:15-20 before. Seems like it always gets pulled out in the middle of a church fight. But the words of Jesus actually give us a clear pathway for reconciliation: If you've got a problem with something or somebody, take care of it privately.

Or as *The Message* translation explains, "If a fellow believer hurts you, go and tell him—work it out *privately* between the two of you. If he listens, you've made a friend. If he won't listen, take one or two others along so that the presence of witnesses will keep things honest, and try again. If he still won't listen, tell the church. If he won't listen to the church, you'll have to start over from scratch, confront him with the need for repentance, and offer again God's forgiving love." [2]

There is a key word in that passage.

Privately.

Jesus was pretty clear about the way you resolve conflict: start by going privately to the person with whom who have the disagreement. We think that directly applies to volunteering.

Volunteers, if you have a problem with your leader or with another volunteer, go *directly* to them and see if you can resolve it, privately.

You would be surprised how many things can be worked out in a peaceful and meaningful way. That's not normal.

Too often, disgruntled and misplaced volunteers do the exact opposite.

Instead of dealing directly and privately, a volunteer-at-war will go to other volunteers recruiting an army, jump over the leader to complain to the senior pastor or walk away in silence leaving others wondering what possibly could have gone wrong.

Who wants to deal with this drama? We don't!

And your leader doesn't either.

All of these little things that we have discussed here distract leaders and volunteers from leading in the right direction.

Your leader needs a cheerleader. Not a Drama Queen.

Your leader needs someone who will build him or her up. Not someone who cuts them down.

YOUR LEADER NEEDS A CHEERLEADER. NOT A DRAMA QUEEN.

Your leader needs someone who will be with him or her when times are good and times are bad. Not someone who bails when the going gets rough.

Your leader needs volunteers to help resolve conflict during emotionally charged times. Not people who stir the pot and cause dissension in the ranks.

We want to challenge you to be a cheerleader. Just don't dress like one unless the script calls for it.

MOOD BOOSTERS

Even if your leader or leaders are uber-joyful people, they are in definite need of encouragement. Often!

Did you know that your leaders love what they do? We are sure of it, because we love what we do. But did you also know that your leaders don't want to talk about what they do during every waking hour of their lives? If you can remember that when interacting with your leader, it will help them see that you recognize their life is bigger than what goes on inside the walls of a church.

In the last section, we talked about all of the things that your leaders have to do in a given week. Their lives can be stressful because of having to navigate all of these different things.

Ministry is one of the only careers that we know of where someone can be a visionary, administrator, media technician, counselor and janitor in the same day.

If you have the opportunity to provide a mood booster for your leader, go ahead and take it!

IF YOU GET A CHANCE, SEND THEM A CARD.

WE WANT TO CHALLENGE YOU TO BE A CHEERLEADER. **JUST DON'T DRESS LIKE ONE UNLESS THE SCRIPT CALLS FOR IT.**

IF YOU GET A CHANCE, TAKE THEM TO LUNCH AND JUST SAY THANKS FOR WHAT THEY DO.

IF YOU GET A CHANCE, TALK TO THEM ABOUT SOMETHING OTHER THAN MINISTRY, BECAUSE THAT IS ALL THEY THINK ABOUT.

If you don't get a chance, go out of your way to get a chance. You'll notice a big difference.

"REBECCA LETS GO"

When I (Adam) came to First Baptist Fort Lauderdale we had one of the largest Vacation Bible Schools in the entire state of Florida. In fact, the big Baptist company that published our VBS materials used our church to showcase to the surrounding churches how to lead a VBS because we did what we did so well. The problem was this: our data told us that VBS was a drop-off service for parents from other churches in the area who wanted their kids to go to multiple Vacation Bible Schools during the summer.

Our core vision wasn't to have a great one-week summer program, but to create a program on the weekends that would reach out to kids and families who aren't already plugged in to a local church. So I joined with our leadership team and made a very difficult decision to stop it. That's right, we stopped VBS at our church, one of the largest ones in the state of Florida.

Before I continue, let me make a statement. I am not anti-VBS. There are many churches which have successful programs that work for their own unique environment. If that works for you, great! It just didn't work for us.

But back to our VBS. Let me tell you about a woman named Rebecca.

She was a volunteer.

SHE WAS THE PERSON WHO HELPED US WITH MARKETING FOR OUR VBS FOR YEARS.

SHE WAS THE PERSON WHO TOOK A LOT OF PRIDE IN HELPING CREATE THE PROGRAM.

SHE WAS THE PERSON WHO DID NOT WANT TO LET THIS PROGRAM GO.

SHE WAS THE PERSON WHO THOUGHT THIS WAS THE BE-ALL AND THE END-ALL OF MINISTRY.

Rebecca had a personal attachment to the VBS program. In fact, three of her four children had come to faith at VBS. They came to authentic faith, too, because Rebecca was such a good parent. Rebecca was not the typical parent who sent her children to every VBS in the tri-state area. She believed that this program we were doing at our church was truly an effective way for reaching the community.

I met with Rebecca after a highly successful VBS my first summer and told her my plans to eliminate this program and put the resources we used into Sunday morning environments so that we could attract younger families and create places they would want to come on the weekends.

I told her that it was not my goal for our church to be on the church-to-church VBS rotating tour. I challenged her to think for a moment about our VBS and who we were really drawing to this event. I explained the priority of reaching those who didn't already have a church and how that could really change families. On and on I explained. But she wasn't buying it.

She could not believe what I was telling her. She stopped and looked at me and said, "Are you out of your mind? You are going to kill the best thing we have going here for kids? For what?"

She wanted to do what she had always done (at least in that moment) and was not happy that I was proposing something different.

I understood. I tried to put myself in her shoes for a minute. Here was a young, childless twentysomething leader (me) who was coming in to disrupt the single most successful week of the children's ministry calendar. I might have been a little upset, too.

Rebecca could have walked out on me if she had been a normal volunteer. She could have left me high and dry. Instead, she left that meeting discouraged but promising to think about it.

The up side of that meeting was that I got to know Rebecca better, and she seemed to be a good fit for one of the volunteer positions in our new weekly environment. I needed a storyteller and a coach to help us manage these new initiatives. When I called and offered her these positions, she kindly declined and indicated that she didn't think that she was going to be able to move forward with our children's ministry and our new direction.

I was disappointed.

But the truth about Rebecca is this: she is someone who is not normal.

Rebecca called me 48 hours later and had this response. "I may not understand why you want to do this, but I trust you. I will accept the new position that you recommended."

She is still a volunteer some six years later, and she and her husband have become some of the best friends Katelyn and I have. Rebecca understood something on that day that we want each of you to understand. You are not going to agree with every decision your leader makes. Odds are, you might not agree with most decisions that your leader makes. That is okay. Do you believe in the vision? If you do, then don't give up. She didn't, and we don't want you too either.

That's honoring the leader.

OFFICE DECORATIONS

They surprised me one morning by decorating my office with different color Post-it notes telling me things I was doing right as their leader. Most of the time in leadership all you hear are the things you messed up, so it was wonderful to hear a few things I was doing right. These notes made my year! I tucked them away in my drawer so I could pull them out and reread them from time to time when things got hard.

1

5 QUIRKY VOLUNTEERS

3

GERMANY

A group of volunteers saved up their money and traveled with our team to Germany for a week for a children's ministry conference there. They took vacation time from work and volunteered from morning to night the whole time. They worked behind the scenes, doing all kinds of tasks to help serve the three thousand children's ministry leaders there. When I would speak, I could see them standing in doorways, waving to me, answering questions, serving attendees by walking their babies around so their parents could be more engaged. The attendees fell in love with our volunteers and watching them soar made me the happiest, proudest leader on the planet.

POST-SURGERY FLOWERS

2

A longtime volunteer named Wayne was an avid Dalia flower grower. I went to see his backyard once and was enthralled with the variety and beauty of huge flowers he was growing there. When his flowers would bloom in the summer, he would bring bouquets and put them in Promiseland for all to appreciate. When I had knee surgery one summer, he came over and planted some of his flowers in a garden for me so that I could have my very own. That gesture meant the world to me. What a sweet man!

THINGS DID FOR SUE

4

CELEBRATING

My co-leader Pat Cimo and I invited the volunteers who had served the longest over to my house one evening. We had planned to celebrate them, but instead we were the ones who got the most out of that night. We asked these lifers in our ministry to tell how and why they had gotten started in children's ministry. The stories they told about how they started and why they stayed were unmistakably the work of our God. We laughed so hard that night. We cried over their life-changing moments. We felt privileged to be on the best faith adventure imaginable on Planet Earth.

5

TOLD ME THEY LOVED ME

One day, I got a card from my volunteers that said nothing more than "We love you" on the front of the card. Inside, all people did was sign their names. We told you small was big.

BIRTHDAY WISHES

For some reason, my volunteers love birthdays. They love to celebrate each others, their family members, and mine! One year my volunteers knew that I collected these Disney things called Vinylmations (basically Mickey Mouse statues that artists draw or paint on). My volunteers got me a blank one and all signed it for my birthday a few years back. I still have it to this day.

1

SCHEDULED A CUP OF COFFEE

One time, a volunteer called me on my cell and asked if he could get together with me for a cup of coffee. If you are a leader, this generally means that someone has a "concern" or someone wants to tell you all of the things that you aren't doing right. We got to the local coffee shop, sat down, and I said, "What's up?" He replied, "I just want to thank you for all that you do. I know you probably don't hear it very often, but that is all I wanted to say." That quick coffee came at a time when I probably needed to hear it the most.

5 QUIRKY VOLUNTEERS

3

CHRISTMAS GIFTS

There is this one volunteer who always buys me a Christmas present! I feel so obligated to return the favor; isn't that what you do? But, she is insistent year after year that I need not give her anything in return because this is just a token of her thanks. And I have to tell you something, every time I get a cup of coffee with the gift card she gives me each year, I remember her leadership and am thankful for the volunteer that she is.

1

DAY 1

4

When we first moved to Fort Lauderdale, the Children's Ministry department was limping along and there were just a few volunteers. I knew I had my hands full. On my first day when I was introduced to the church, we were hanging out in the lobby and a younger couple came up to us with a very clear goal: to help. Their names were Kristin and Tim. They said, "Look, we don't know you or what you want to do with this, but we want to help you do it." I was shocked. They were the first people to sign up to help me launch this strategy, and are still volunteering to this day. That might be the most special thing yet.

2

THINGS
DID FOR ADAM

5

THEY KEEP IN TOUCH

Volunteers that I had the privilege of leading years ago still keep in touch with me, and I love it. They will come to hang out when I am back in town, they will text and call, and they continually fill my bucket up by reminding me how much of an impact our ministry had on them. I care so much about those who give themselves to a cause, specifically one that I am helping to lead. The fact that these people still take time out of their busy lives to stay in touch means a lot.

CHA

PTER

6

REPLACE YOURSELF

Nothing could be quirkier than **a leader who is already replacing himself or herself with someone even better.**

THIS NEXT QUIRK WILL SURPRISE YOU.

IT WILL COME UP WHEN YOU LEAST EXPECT IT.

IT'S BOTH AWFUL AND AWESOME AT THE SAME TIME.

Curious?

You should have looked at the title of this chapter, silly.

THIS QUIRK CREATES SOME TURMOIL INSIDE EVERY NOT NORMAL VOLUNTEER.

YOUR CHARACTER AND PERSONAL FAITH WILL GET TESTED.

THESE MOMENTS SURFACE WHEN WE START THINKING ABOUT THE FUTURE.

Your future.

Believe it or not, there will come a day when you feel like you've found your zone. You are hitting your stride, feeling comfortable, like you've finally gotten your arms wrapped around this thing that you're doing.

And then…..

A NEW OPPORTUNITY OPENS UP FOR YOU.

ANOTHER VOLUNTEER WANTS TO DO WHAT YOU ARE DOING.

SOMEONE COMES ALONG WHO CAN DO THIS BETTER THAN YOU.

THE GROWTH OF YOUR CAUSE GETS BIGGER AND YOU NEED MORE RECRUITS.

WHAT DOES A NOT NORMAL VOLUNTEER NEED TO DO?

Replace yourself.

This topic is personal, deep and can press us to examine what is going on inside of our own heart and mind.

You probably never ever imagined having this discussion when you walked into your volunteering spot that first day, did you?

Especially after we've just spent the first five chapters telling you how important it is to start volunteering, own what you do and don't rent what you do, honor the leader, and more, and now we're telling you to move on? Kind of, yes.

Allow us to explain before you deposit this book in the nearest trash receptacle.

Think back over all of the jobs you have had throughout your life. It could be when you were in high school and you were flipping burgers, or it could be your first executive position with a corporation. This truth is true about each and every job: someone else is doing that job now.

And as much as you love what you are doing now at your church, you innately realize you won't be doing it forever. Change is something all of us can count on happening, and it will happen to you as a volunteer as well. And it's a good thing, because change helps us keep growing into the "what's next" in our future.

You are where you are now for a time and a season, but what you are a part of is bigger than you and your service. Somewhere up ahead, when the time is right, your next quirky step will be to move on to something else and allow someone new to do what you are doing now. (And they might even be better at it!)

We said this would be difficult.

And yes, we are saying that you should, when the time is right…

ALLOW YOUR TEENAGERS TO GET TO KNOW A NEW SMALL GROUP LEADER.

GIVE UP CONTROL OF THE AUDIO BOARD TO LET SOMEONE ELSE LEARN.

MOVE UP IN LEADERSHIP TO LEAD VOLUNTEERS RATHER THAN GREETING AT THE DOOR.

LOOK FOR SOMEONE NEW TO ADD TO YOUR TEAM.

You should be working toward this goal all of the time.

I (Adam) am pretty blunt with my volunteers that I am not going to be around forever. Now, I might be around for a little while, but I know I am not going to do what I am doing right now forever. Let us take a moment to state that we think leaders should stay around as long as they can. There is something special that happens when leaders stay for an extended period of time. With that said, we know leaders aren't around forever. So, I give our volunteers a lot of authority. I remember our large group volunteers asking me, "Why are you letting me take the stage so much?" I replied, "Because one day you will get good enough that you can run this whole thing. Maybe you can even take my job and I can go find something else to do."

Side note here, my favorite job of all time was working at CVS Pharmacy. I LOVED "Truck Day" when the truck with all of the stock merchandise would come in, because I loved stocking the shampoo aisle. That was where I was assigned. By the end of that day, you had never seen such a beautiful display of Pantene Pro V. I was the best.

I tell you that because some day, if someone like this awesome young leader comes in and takes my job, I would love to spend one day a week going back and stocking the shampoo aisle! It was so relaxing.

If we aren't willing to let go of the things we worked so hard to build, then we are just in it for us, and that attitude will never win. Not normal volunteers understand that.

One day, someone will come in who

WANTS TO DO WHAT YOU ARE DOING

HAS NEW IDEAS

WANTS TO CHANGE THINGS

IS READY FOR THEIR NEXT STEP

All of those things are good. And you, as a not normal volunteer, should not only welcome it to happen, you should help facilitate it.

We heard a story about a situation in a student ministry that helps illustrate this point.

IF WE AREN'T WILLING TO LET GO OF THE THINGS WE WORKED SO HARD TO BUILD, THEN **WE ARE JUST IN IT FOR US,** AND THAT ATTITUDE WILL NEVER WIN. NOT NORMAL VOLUNTEERS UNDERSTAND THAT.

There was a couple that had traditionally been the "senior class" small group leaders. The couple was awesome. They invested in these kids' lives for years and years and kids who came through this small group had a great foundation to enter college. Well, this couple had done this for a long time and didn't really even think about what it might look like to be replaced or to move on.

The church was beginning to implement more of a Lead Small strategy and small group leaders in high school were committing to serving all four years with their teenagers. Sure enough, there was a small group leader who started with her freshman girls and three years later was ready to move up with them all the way to their senior year. Well, when the time came, the tenured couple was not having any of it.

The couple didn't understand what it meant to allow yourself to be replaced so that a greater good can happen where you serve. Their leader had to step into an ugly situation because this particular principle wasn't understood or embraced. That's what normal can look like. We don't want that for incredible volunteers like you.

Another thing to consider is that most ministries need additional volunteers from time to time as the ministry grows. Not normal volunteers are aware of that, and actively look at people in their own circle of influence that they can invite into the mix. If you believe in the vision of what you are doing, there is nobody better to help replace yourself than you.

YOU UNDERSTAND WHAT TYPE OF LEADER IS NECESSARY TO DO WHAT YOU DO.

YOU UNDERSTAND HOW MUCH GOES INTO THE POSITION.

YOU CAN DESCRIBE THE DETAILS OF IT TO THE NEXT PERSON.

YOU UNDERSTAND AND KNOW THE KIDS AND TEENAGERS YOU LEAD.

YOU KNOW THE IMPACT THAT CAN HAPPEN FROM FIRST-HAND EXPERIENCE.

Who better to hand these things off to the next person than you? The answer is, there isn't anyone better.

Replacing yourself as a volunteer is essential for growth to happen wherever you serve. It's important for you too. It gives you a chance to grow into your next role, so you continue to grow and be challenged. And it's important to bring new volunteers in so we can keep enlarging our impact towards the cause that we care about.

But there are a few essential things you need to know as you look to do this as a not normal volunteer.

LET GO

It's normal for all of us to want to dig our heels in, stay where we are, feeling afraid of what the future might hold next for us. After all, it took a lot for us to jump in and get this far. Once we are there, we want to hold on tight to the present, and instead, we need to loosen the grip on our current situation one finger at a time, and start to let go.

LET GO OF WHAT YOU WANT.

LET GO OF YOUR CURRENT ROLE.

LET GO OF CONTROLLING YOUR FUTURE.

We know that is hard to do. Especially when you love something that you do, or even more important, the people you get to volunteer with. Sometimes our identity even gets connected to what we are doing or where we are serving. We become known as the "best communicator" or the "number one small group leader" or "the unstoppable administrator." We like hearing others say that to us. And there's nothing wrong with that, unless you won't move on to your next step because you are too wrapped up in that identity to give it up.

We get comfortable with the way things are now. We love the people we serve with now. We don't want anyone to rock our boat. But the cause might need someone with different skills, or the growth requires more people, or a new strategy is coming into place so that the future can have even more impact. Your boat might need to get rocked for really great reasons!

There comes a time in every not normal volunteer's life when it is time to move on to something else. As you begin the process of letting go, expect an emotional reaction to accompany your decision as you start to reminisce about all of the good times in the past.

There are definitely some great things that you should hold onto: the amazing memories that you shared with others, the moments that you shared when you first signed up for this position and entered this space for the first time and the relationships you've formed so far

Here is the thing. In every change, a win and a loss are at stake. There is a trade-off.

Change is personal for all of us because in every change, we lose something and gain something else. Take time to understand the loss that you are feeling. Think about what you will miss. Appreciate the people you worked alongside and tell them you will miss them. Take a little time to let yourself process what will be going away. Often we want to just skip over this part, and we struggle to get to the new future immediately. Give it some time. Then, decide what you want to do next. This is all a part of the process related to letting go.

A not normal volunteer named Bridget walked through this lesson as a middle school small group leader.

Bridget had a group of ten girls that had been with her since sixth grade. What had started out as an awkward, rather shy group of girls had turned into a very tight-knit small group.

They had great conversations over time. Bridget got to know these girls and their parents really well. She had talked these girls off the ledge many times during fights with their parents over the past three years. There had been lots of drama over friends, faith, boys, curfew, computer rights and grades.

Bridget, having had three kids of her own, navigated these situations the best she could. She certainly didn't get it right every time. She just tried to help her girls build strong relationships with their parents, knowing that this was a season of great ups and downs emotionally for all of them. Both trusted her advice and wisdom. Bridget was authentic and transparent and they liked that about her. She was the real deal when it comes to living out faith day to day.

Bridget remembered the small things and checked in with her girls regularly to see how they were doing. Her girls loved texting with her. She threw great sleepovers when she could; they all looked forward to hanging out at her house. She taught them how to make homemade pizza, and every year they baked Christmas cookies together. Bridget was an accomplished aerobics trainer, and knew all kinds of great exercise tips. They were fascinated and eager to learn.

She was also a football fanatic. Bridget actually took her girls to her college homecoming game so they could experience what it was like. She wanted to give them something to look forward to academically.

The girls were even invited to Bridget's daughter's wedding. They took a photo together at the reception. Bridget sent each girl a copy of the photo with something handwritten from her on the photo frame to mark that moment together.

Bridget was a rock star small group leader with middle schoolers.

So imagine the pressure she faced when the girls were graduating from eighth grade, and getting ready to enter the high school ministry. The girls insisted that she move up with them for four more years. Their parents begged her to stick with them for four more years. And that's what Bridget planned to do.

Until she met with her ministry leader Mark, and he said............ no.

Whhhhhhaaaaattttt? Yep, he had a different strategy in mind.

And it was a good one.

He told Bridget that she was a champion middle school small group leader. It was obvious to everyone on their team that she had a very special gift with this age group. People like Bridget do not come along every day in middle school ministry.

He asked Bridget to stay put and take on a brand new sixth grade girls group in September, and give them the same terrific experience for three years. She was shocked at his request, having never considered starting over with another group.

Mark gently told Bridget that it was time for her to let go of this group and allow them to be led by someone else for the next four years. It was time to give another leader a chance to speak into these girls' lives and help grow their faith from a fresh perspective.

It was the right thing to do. After Bridget thought about it, it made perfect sense.

But that didn't mean it was easy.

THERE WERE A LOT OF TEARS.

THERE WERE MIXED FEELINGS ALL AROUND: WITH THE GIRLS, PARENTS AND BRIDGET.

THERE WAS SOME PROCESSING THAT NEEDED TO HAPPEN BEFORE THEY COULD EMBRACE A NEW FUTURE.

But not normal Bridget walked through it all, confident that her leader was right.

Months later, she met her brand new group of awkward sixth grade girls. She asked them to share their stories thus far, and as they started talking. Bridget found herself getting a little excited all over again. She thought about their potential. She realized that she was going to be able to impact the lives of ten more girls!

At the end of the day, every decision that you make has its plusses and minuses. But some of the healthiest and most constructive decisions in our life will come when we decide to go through the painful process of letting go of something good to do something better.

Think about this for a second. What is next for you?

Is it moving up from running the sound board once a month to leading the entire tech team once a month? That would mean that someone else is directly running the sound board. Can you do that?

Is it time to move on from being a greeter to being someone who teaches the Bible message? You have enjoyed welcoming families, but are always curious as to what it would take to get on stage and communicate with kids or teenagers. That would mean someone else is the friendly face at the door welcoming families as they arrive. Can you do that?

Is it moving from being a small group leader to being a coach? Maybe it is time to take what you have learned about being a small group leader and pass that wisdom along to others so they can succeed at investing in the lives of a few. That would mean someone else will be the small group leader of the kids you have led for the past few years. Can you do that?

What is next for you?

You won't experience it if your grip is so tight around what you currently have that you can't loosen it to see what is next.

For the not normal volunteer, be ready to just let go.

LET GO OF THE FEAR

Imagine this. Your leader comes to you and says, "I have a new opportunity for you. After watching you serve for the past few years, I have a different position that I think you would excel in. I have someone that I would like you to apprentice to take your current position. This will happen as

YOU WON'T EXPERIENCE
IT IF YOUR GRIP IS SO
TIGHT AROUND WHAT YOU
CURRENTLY HAVE **THAT
YOU CAN'T LOOSEN IT TO
SEE WHAT IS NEXT.**

we transition into the next school year in about two months. Interested?"

What is it about that statement that strikes fear in us?

Thoughts race through our mind like…

"What? Am I not doing a good enough job at my position now and you are replacing me?"

"If you think I am not capable of doing this, I would appreciate you just telling me rather than beating around the bush."

"I knew it. I am inadequate. God was wrong when He told me to do this. I'm done."

The fact of the matter is, it is none of those things. But for whatever reason those feelings emerge…call it human nature, our own fear, or us watching too much daily news. We usually think first that someone is out to get us or that someone doesn't have our best interest at heart.

Whether it is true or not, we get wrapped up in our own blanket of fear. And then we think the worst.

So, we have a response for every not normal volunteer: Let go of the fear.

We can remember a time in both of our careers when we were afraid of the littlest things. They could have been as small as someone saying to us…

"I really think this is a church and you need to dress more appropriately" (Meaning, please stop wearing flip-flops. I think you look like an idiot.)

"I don't really like today's lesson. Can't you come up with something a bit deeper or more spiritual?" (Meaning, you have a shallow faith. I'm not sure you are the person that should teach others.)

"I'm not digging the way you presented that topic to a group of teenage boys. I think it could have been done in a different way." (Meaning, you are way too entertaining as a communicator. I think you should be boring as dirt. That's the way I learned the Bible and if it was good enough forty years ago it's good enough now.)

These are just a few of the things (and trust us, we would need another entire book to review them all) that we have heard throughout our careers.

It could have come from a lead pastor or from someone we managed or it could have come from a volunteer.

Why do any of us take moments like these so hard?

Because all of us are so passionate about what we do! Especially incredible volunteers like you.

You lose countless hours of sleep, spend time away from your families or friends, and give your blood, sweat, and tears to help achieve these goals! No wonder we take things personally - increasing our fear and insecurity about who we are.

The point is, even though it might be personal, not normal volunteers can't look at it that way.

The thing that you are serving for is bigger than you. The very thing that you signed up to contribute to and to help move forward is more important than all of your insecurity issues.

Society has an anxiety complex and it doesn't go away at church, or wherever you serve.

You see it when you're texting someone and they don't text back right away. Ever done that?

More than likely the person is either in the restroom (okay, that's not a good excuse because most people take their phone to the restroom with them), or they just aren't near it at that moment. But if a person doesn't text back right away we generally think…

"Oh no, they're mad at me. What did I do?"

We heard a story about a woman named Yvonne who was in charge of large group for kids during the church hour on a Sunday morning. She was awesome. She served as the producer twice a month. This church was in the process of launching their family experience and they needed the very best in charge of family experience. They needed someone to call cues, organize rehearsals, and to make sure all of the moving pieces fit together so that this environment could go off without a hitch. Yvonne was the person that the family ministry wanted to run family experience. So, they approached her.

The team thought that Yvonne would be super-excited about this new opportunity. After the pitch to Yvonne from the team, Yvonne's reaction was kind of surprising to them. She said, "I'm being replaced? How could you do this to me? I love what I do when I produce large group. Did I mess something up, am I being fired? I don't think I can give it up!"

Yvonne's reaction was the same reaction many of us have. She jumped to conclusions, assuming the worst instead of the best right from the get go. She didn't even hear what the team was trying to say to her about how good they thought she was. She got upset, and then shut down emotionally after the conversation took place.

After awhile, Yvonne sat down with her leader and admitted her fear of failing. She actually let go of her fear enough to begin to hear what opportunity she was being asked to take. She realized that this was because she had been doing a great job up to this point and was being challenged to grow some more in a brand new role. Her leader encouraged her to let go of her fear and try the new position out. Turns out, she loved producing family experience. It was totally her jam. She loves it, excels at it, and has made that environment very special for families.

She also learned that not normal volunteers let go of the fear. How quirky is that?

LOOK AHEAD

Reminiscing about good times in our lives is something that all of us should do.

We can remember some of the best moments in our entire lives happening in ministry, particularly at places where we no longer serve. It's fun to look back and remember them from time to time.

THE FUNNY MOMENTS WHERE STUFF FELL DOWN, BLEW UP OR WENT AWRY

SUPERNATURAL MOMENTS WHERE LIFE CHANGE HAPPENED IN SPITE OF US, ACTUALLY

PRAYERS THAT GOT ANSWERED IN A BIG WAY

STAFF MEMBERS WHO BECAME FAMILY

TIMES WHEN THE MINISTRY ALMOST CAME APART FOR ONE REASON OR ANOTHER

TIMES WHEN WE ALMOST CAME APART FOR ONE REASON OR ANOTHER

SECURITY CHANGES THAT MADE PARENTS MAD THOUGH WE WERE TRYING TO PROTECT THEIR KIDS

STUPID CREATIVE STUFF WE TRIED THAT DIDN'T WORK AT ALL

JOKES KIDS TOLD US THAT WEREN'T EVEN FUNNY

THE NUMBER OF TIMES SOMEONE LOST THEIR COOKIES DURING FLU SEASON

HOW WE THOUGHT THESE WERE CERTAINLY OUR BEST DAYS

Looking back is great because those memories help us see how far we've come in our journey. But we don't want you to get so wrapped up in what once was that you can't see how bright the future is. We want you to realize that you are living in your best days right now, in this season.

And there's still more to come your way.

Not normal volunteers have to look ahead. Incredible people like you cannot afford to get stuck living in the past.

Has that ever happened to you in your life?

Whether that is a

PREVIOUS RELATIONSHIP

PREVIOUS JOB

PREVIOUS CITY

PREVIOUS TIME IN YOUR LIFE

When you understand this principle of not looking back, you understand that you have so much more to gain as you experience this. The future is filled with uncharted waters and new adventures as you keep looking ahead to what's next.

Had Tina only looked back on her time as a nursery worker, she never would have taken that position as a second grade girls small group leader. She would have missed getting to know Rowan and her single dad, and playing a part in him coming to faith.

Had Chip only looked back on his time playing in the worship band in high school, he never would have started to teach large group in middle school. He would have missed the opportunity to teach middle schoolers something that changed the way they looked at God.

Had Jennifer only looked back on her time as a small group leader, she would have missed leading a missions trip to Nicaragua. She wouldn't have found her passion for the poor if she hadn't signed up for something new.

Had we only looked back on our previous careers, we would never be writing this book today.

In fact, this principle applies to a lot more than just volunteering (but that is another book for another time).

One of my (Adam) favorite memories from my church in Michigan was a whitewater rafting coaches trip that we took in West Virginia. We had sixteen of our coaches go on this trip and it was a ball of fun. We didn't do a lot of training or going over material for the year. This was simply to have fun. Why? Because we believe that fun is one of the most important things that volunteers can have together. Remember, people like parties!

One night on the trip a guy who was in charge of recruiting other volunteers and I were sitting around the campfire and he said something that really made me think about my future in a different way. He said to me, "You know, it really doesn't get any better than this, and it might never be better than this!" I remember protesting to myself, "It has to get better than this. It always has to get better than where we are currently."

If you think about the past more than you think about the future you are squelching your potential to grow. You will miss the good ole days that are still up ahead. You might miss an incredible relationship still to be encountered, or the opportunity of a lifetime to take you where you've never been before.

Moments can be great. The future can be even better.

I remember that trip very fondly and think of those people often. In fact, I still keep in touch with many of them. But my thoughts are not there each and every day any longer because I am busy dreaming about and thinking about what's here and now, and what is next.

We don't want you to miss a single opportunity God has in store for you up ahead. So please don't get anchored in the past.

Remember. You. Are. A. Not. Normal Volunteer. Look ahead.

"CHRISTY GETS REPLACED. TWICE!"

Christy is one of those not normal volunteers that leaders see once, maybe twice in their ministry career.

See, Christy used to run the elementary ministry department for years when no one else was around. Basically, she was a volunteer and then graciously offered her services as part-time staff to help run the program because the church didn't want to pay someone full-time at that point.

Christy was in her sixties. She begged the church to hire a children's pastor.

Begged them.

She knew she wasn't the person to run this thing long-term. She wanted a younger leader to come in and to steer this ship in a different direction. As soon as the church found a full-time leader, Christy gladly resigned and became a volunteer again. It was a smooth transition of power. How often do you hear about the opposite these days?

Christy served in many capacities, but as things changed, she landed in her position of small group coach. She loved it. She loved leading and investing in the lives of small group leaders. She would send weekly e-mails, lead the weekly huddle meetings, and loved standing in the back of the theatre and watching the large group time.

Christy served in this new role for five years after she left the staff position. Five years! We love what happens when people invest time like that; it really can change the course of a church's history.

One day, Christy approached her leader with some news. Christy's only daughter and her husband and their two very young children were moving to North Carolina. Christy was struggling as to what the right decision was, to stay or to go.

Her leader said something that he always said to his volunteers, "Your family is first. That's what we tell our families who come here, and that is what we believe. You know what is right."

Christy and her husband began making plans to move to the Tar Heel State.

The one thing that wasn't in place was Christy's replacement, and she knew it. She knew that one of the things during her volunteer career that she had not planned for was a transition. So, she did what any over and above person would do. She met with the leadership of the department and said, "Gang, I've got five months left here. That is way more than enough time to find replacements for me, train them, and set them free. I want to be a part of that."

So, sure enough, Christy went on the hunt for the right people to replace herself with. She brought suggestions of ideal candidates and she went after them. And, if you know anything about coaches, they aren't easy positions to fill. Coaches have to be of the right mindset and have a different set of skills than other volunteers.

After a few weeks of searching, phone calls, cups of coffee and observation, Christy had replaced herself with not only one but TWO new volunteers. Totally quirky!

It was time to bust her position into two so that a "Lead Small" culture could be advanced. Not only were these people in place within weeks of Christy announcing that she was going to be leaving, but they then had over three months of observation to see what Christy did and how she led. They could decide what they liked and what they wanted to do differently.

The most emotional time was when Christy said goodbye. It was a sweet time of prayer, remembering some great times under her leadership. There wasn't a dry eye in the room. In that moment, Christy was able to introduce her team, the team she had led for years and years, to their new leaders. It was a true "passing of the torch" and it could not have gone smoother. The new coaches were welcomed and loved because of what Christy did to replace herself.

1

WAITRESS

I started out as a waitress at Don Roth's Dinner Restaurant. I did this for two years while I was in college. I made more there per hour than I did when I took my first ministry job. The food was very high end. Can you imagine how great it smelled to someone who had to eat school cafeteria food every day? One night, a party of ten came in to celebrate a couple's anniversary. While bringing them a Flaming Baked Alaska, I accidentally set my hair on fire. I haven't wanted to waitress since.

2

ADMINISTRATIVE ASSISTANT

One summer, I worked in downtown Chicago for an insurance company at this high-rise office building. I was hired to answer phones for five bosses who treated me like their daughter. I helped one guy balance his checkbook each month, another needed me to take his clients to lunch and schmooze with them. I loved the variety of people and tasks I had with this job, but I discovered that I have no passion about the insurance business.

AVON SALESPERSON

3

I took a shot at this one summer during college. I was not good at this. I loved the product, but discovered I hated selling. I didn't want to force anyone. I didn't want to impose. I was not at all good. I think I earned $200 that summer, mainly because my mother and my mother-in-law bought from me every time out of sheer pity for me. No future in sales for me!

SCHOOL TEACHER

4

I loved being a classroom teacher over the ten years I worked in public schools. I found my sweet spot. The only reason I ever left was because of a pastor who challenged me to take the best of what I had learned in the classroom and use it for greater Kingdom impact inside the local church. When I look back, I can't imagine what I would have missed if I hadn't said yes to my next step.

CHILDREN'S MINISTRY DIRECTOR

I served at Willow Creek Community Church with a dream team of staff and volunteers. My best friends were there, the kind you do life and ministry with at the same time. I was given opportunities to soar there as a woman in leadership like very few experience in most local churches. I thought I would be a lifer at Willow Creek. But God used Reggie Joiner to lead me to a new Orange-colored adventure, so I took the next step and now I get to be part of so many wonderful family ministries around the world.

5

PIZZA MAKER

When I was in high school, I worked at a place named "Marco's Pizza" in Lambertville, Michigan. I loved seeing the fresh dough come out of the cooler and get formed into this beautiful creation with whatever toppings the customer wanted. The best part? For me, it was the cut table. I loved cutting it perfectly into eight slices. I took pride in it, and I was super fast.

PHARMACY CLERK

My all-time favorite job. That's right! This was magic. It just so happened that the right people were in the right place at the right time. There was nothing particularly amazing about this job, other than I LOVED stocking the shampoo aisle! About 90 minutes before we closed, the store manager would ask, "Can you go around and front and face (straighten merchandise) the entire store?" Heaven!

WAITER AT A BAR AND GRILLE

I worked at a bar and grille when I was in college to pay my way through school, and because of this I was able to graduate debt-free. On the opening night, my best friend came in to celebrate the grand opening, and I spilled a drink on him. He reminds me of it to this day.

COFFEE BARISTA

I hated this job. It was brutal. This was at a local coffee shop to make a few extra bucks and it was terrible. The worst part of it, for me, was consistently cleaning the machines that we used to make the specialty coffee drinks. Those things never came clean, no matter how many times you cleaned them. Keep that in mind next time you order a double latte with extra foam.

4

CHILDREN'S PASTOR

This was the hardest job I have ever left. I was Children's Pastor at CrossRoads Community Church in Ottawa Lake, Michigan. The people I served with were my best friends. The best man in my wedding, my sister, the person who has had the greatest impact my life I met on my first day as a volunteer.... I still miss these people to this day (and if you are one of them reading this, know that I miss you.) But, now I need to take my own advice and stop looking back, so I can look on to the future.

5

CHA

PTER

7

YOU CAN'T ALWAYS SEE IT

The seventh quirk? **Dream big and understand reality.**

Isn't it wonderful how quickly we can get stuff today?

We can...

GET DIRECTIONS IN A FRACTION OF A SECOND

STREAM MOVIES ON OUR TV IN MINUTES

BUY FROM STORES WITH SAME-DAY SERVICE

ORDER JIMMY JOHNS AND IT APPEARS TO HAVE ALREADY BEEN WAITING AT OUR DOOR

RESERVE A TABLE AT A HOT RESTAURANT IN AN INSTANT

GET HEARTBURN IN SHORT ORDER AFTER MEXICAN FOOD

There are definite advantages to being able to get what we want quickly. After all, our lives are hyperbusy, so we appreciate not having our time wasted. We want what we want and we want it now. We don't have time to wait around.

We race to get. . . . .

THE NEWEST IPHONE VERSION

THE FASTEST FASTPASS AT DISNEY WORLD

THE HOTTEST CONCERT TICKETS

THE NUMBER ONE CHRISTMAS TOY

IN TO SEE THE LATEST MOVIE RELEASE

THE BRAND NEW VIDEO GAME

It's easy to see why we would step into our volunteer role and expect a serving FastPass to accomplish our goal!

When we see something that is unjust, or someone who needs help, we want to fix it or THEM right away. Instant results. Bada Bing, Bada Boom! The truth is that it doesn't happen that fast.

And when THAT doesn't happen, then THIS happens:

Linda quit volunteering with toddlers because it didn't seem important.

Tom stopped showing up for middle schoolers because no one was changing.

Bob told his coach that he didn't feel like a very good special needs leader.

Carole gave up her high school girls group because they wanted to talk more about boys than a relationship with God.

Jeremy emailed his resignation saying that holding babies on Sunday didn't seem very spiritual.

Seems pretty normal to us — but then we have to ask a question.

What went wrong?

In each of these situations, volunteers signed up to help build faith in the next generation. Week after week they showed up but didn't see any tangible results. There wasn't anything they could point to that would validate the time they were spending each week. So they assumed what they were doing wasn't significant and they quit.

To keep that from happening to you, there are some things that will help you go bigger and serve over and above.

DON'T ASSUME IT'S NOT HAPPENING

We get so used to getting things quickly that we forget about the really great things that can't be done in an instant. Waiting is required because results don't come overnight.

Like. . . . .

FRIENDSHIPS

LEARNING HOW TO DRIVE

GETTING OUT OF DEBT

PURSUING AN EDUCATION

STARTING A COMPANY

BUILDING A FAITH THAT LASTS

GROWING A MARRIAGE

RAISING CHILDREN

WRITING A BOOK :)

It takes lots of patience to accomplish any one of those things. But wouldn't we agree that they are worth it? Just because we don't see immediate results, we have to be very

WE GET SO USED TO GETTING THINGS QUICKLY THAT **WE FORGET ABOUT THE REALLY GREAT THINGS THAT CAN'T BE DONE IN AN INSTANT.**

careful to guard our hearts and minds against the idea that we assume it isn't happening.

Remember what they (we don't know who "they" is, but we reference them anyway) say about the word assume… If you assume it (our editor just made us stop writing. Moving on…)

We have to be willing to go the distance in order to get the satisfaction that comes after all the time and effort. It's the old "Rome wasn't built in a day" idea.

BUT. . . . .

WE SOMETIMES FORGET THE IDEA OF PROCESS WHEN WE VOLUNTEER. WE WANT LIFE CHANGE AND SPIRITUAL GROWTH, AND WE WANT IT NOW.

WE WANT THE BABIES WE SERVE TO HAVE MORE LIFE CHANGE THAN DIAPER CHANGE.

WE WANT THE FIVE-YEAR-OLDS TO SIT LIKE STATUES SOAKING UP OUR BIBLICAL WISDOM.

WE WANT THE MIDDLE SCHOOLERS TO DECIDE TO MAKE FAITH THEIR OWN RIGHT NOW.

WE WANT EVERY HIGH SCHOOL STUDENT TO BE A SURPRISINGLY SERIOUS PEER LEADER WHO HAS JUST ENOUGH COOL TO WIN EVERYBODY ELSE OVER TOO.

Wouldn't that be awesome? Just think about how significant volunteers would feel if it really worked that way. Every volunteer would walk away feeling fulfilled every time they served.

Who wouldn't love that?

Well, God, for one. That wasn't what He had in mind.

He designed each child uniquely, knowing that each one will grow at their own pace.

He knew that middle schoolers would have to process through their doubts in order to have a faith that is their own.

He knew that teenagers would learn how to trust Him more as they struggled to figure out the next step in their lives.

His idea was for you and me to walk alongside them, loving them through their ups and downs, showing them who God is by the way we care for them.

Let's face it. Building faith in the next generation takes time. There aren't going to be immediate results. Learning, processing and trusting God is going to take a lifetime for each child to grow through, just like it did for us. We're going to have to be patient.

But do you want to hear the good news? **We get a front row seat to watch it and participate in it during their first twenty-one years.** That's an incredible opportunity when you think about it. Keep that in mind as you serve week to week.

We are all tempted to assume that if we can't see the result, then it must not be happening. We want some proof, something concrete that we can point to after volunteering awhile and say THERE IT IS. That's what I've been accomplishing. See?

It's kind of ironic, really, because we are surrounded by things that we put our trust in all day long even though we cannot see how they work.

Like. . . . .

PLANTING SEEDS THAT TURN INTO FLOWERS

CATERPILLARS COMING OUT OF THE COCOON AS BUTTERFLIES

HUGE HEAVY AIRPLANES FLYING IN THE SKY WITHOUT STRINGS

ELECTRICITY

WIFI

GRAVITY

But, that doesn't stop us from planting gardens, flying on planes, or using wifi, does it?

We trust these things to work, even though we can't see how they work. Could it be that when we are with a group of kids that things might be happening, even though we can't see it?

A small group leader named Kiki served regularly in the four-year-old room. This age group gave her so much joy. She loved spending time with them. But lately she left wondering if anything significant was happening with her small group kids. All she could see was that…

THEIR ATTENTION WANDERED

EACH ONE HAD THEIR OWN STORIES TO TELL

SOME HAD TROUBLE SITTING

OTHERS JUST WANTED TO PLAY

A FEW MISSED MOM OR DAD

Couple that with simple activities, quick prayers, and bite-sized content and it's easy to understand how Kiki began to confuse simple with insignificant.

An email from Ellary's mom changed her perspective.

Dear Miss Kiki,

I just had to tell you how much of an impact you are having on our daughter Ellary. We feel like you are a part of our family. You don't know this, but when Ellary is at home playing, she pretends to be YOU.

She carefully lines up her dolls and stuffed animals all around her, and then places a pencil behind her right ear as she starts to talk to them.

She welcomes each one with a great big smile.

Opens up her little Bible and tells them a story.

Prays for each one by name.

Passes out a little snack in a Dixie cup.

Hugs them goodbye before they leave.

Just. Like. You.

We want you to know that our family appreciates you more than we can ever say. Thank you for Investing in our daughter.

Mr. and Mrs. Wilder

Kiki wasn't normal, and had she not gotten this letter she would have never known how much impact she was having.

The surface of a preschool child never tells the whole story. There's always learning happening that we don't see. Experts tell us they are soaking up learning like sponges everywhere they go. During the first five years they will learn more than at any other time in their lives.

So, even if you can't see the learning, we dare not assume it's not happening.

Sometimes, you can be surprised by someone's growth as you get a glimpse of them further down the line.

There is another preschool leader we know who has experienced this. Her name is Kathy. She gets to know most all of the regularly attending little ones over the four years they are in her department.

Kathy's friend Jessica invited her to come to a Baptism Celebration event for 10-year-olds and their parents. These kids wanted to be baptized and were able to invite close family and friends to come with them. Kathy knew Jessica's son, so she definitely wanted to show up for him and celebrate this special day with their family.

While Kathy was waiting for her young friend to get baptized, she was able to see all of the other kids on the stage also. To her surprise, these were kids that she knew. She had seen them their first four years. But after that, she hadn't seen most of them since. Until today.

She felt such a sense of wonder as she thought about how far each one of them had come.

She was overcome by gratefulness that she had been able to know them and their parents from their earliest days at their church.

She felt privileged to have played a small part in helping them get to this place today.

It kind of made all of the Sundays worth getting up for: all of the cold rainy ones, all of the chaotic ones, all of the holiday ones.

To see the results of her service six years later was mind-blowing to her.

Just because you can't see any immediate results of change, spiritual growth, or whatever you are looking to see in the capacity you serve, please don't assume it's not happening. It messes with your psyche to have this idea floating around in your brain. The one that says, "Maybe what I am doing isn't making any sort of difference at all." That thought needs to fly far away and needs to never touch the ground again. When you understand that things actually are happening and you do make a difference, you will serve in a different way.

One day, you're going to be surprised, just like not normal Kiki and Kathy were.

BELIEVE IN THE FUTURE

My (Sue's) husband Rick and I recently moved to a fixer-upper located on Lake Lanier, a giant manmade reservoir about an hour north of Atlanta. We both love living on the water, and all of the activities that go with it. One night this past summer, we found an island where we could beach our pontoon boat and swim. The water was like glass with hardly a breeze to be felt. It was the perfect time for skipping stones on the water.

We had a competition to see who could get the most skips, throwing rock after rock off of the beach. I was fixated on the ripples caused as the stones hit the water. It reminded me of the kind of person I want to be.

I want to invest in the future, leaving all kinds of ripples behind when my time here is done. Building faith into leaders, who build faith into volunteers, who build faith in the next generation is what I want to be about. I want to leave behind a legacy in people that will far outlast my time here.

Because I believe in the future.

Normal people live for the here and now, focusing all of their energy and resources on their own needs and interests.

But not us. You are not normal, and neither are we.

We think you believe in the future too. Hopefully, we are all aware that this life isn't all there is. That means we have to think about what happens next, after this life.

For those of us following Jesus, we are looking forward to Heaven one day. There, we will be rewarded for every not normal thing we have done to love and serve someone else by the One who asked us to do it. For real. Check this out....

"Our Father, who sees in secret, will reward us on that day" (Galatians 6:7).

Isn't that amazing? How cool is that Awards Ceremony going to be? God is going to weigh in on what we were giving ourselves to accomplish. It is going to be awesome. A don't-miss event. One beyond what we can even imagine.

But it's easy to forget about what's up ahead. We get discouraged by the normal here and now. Volunteering can feel like the longest, most arduous journey at times.

Maybe it's because volunteering happens mostly behind the scenes.

Houses get built, wells get dug and shelters get run without a lot of people knowing about it. These are usually not buzzworthy events in the press.

Many serving moments happen without recognition, thanks or appreciation.

Often it happens in less than ideal environments: church basements, old gymnasiums, mobile trailers or on shaky church vans.

It's almost as if God knew how we would feel in our role. Like He has ultimate wisdom in this or something, or maybe He was there Himself one day a few thousand years ago.

Add to that the reality that....

The majority of time we don't get to hear the rest of each person's faith story.

WE JUST ENCOUNTERED THEM FOR A WEEK AT THE SHELTER.

WE ONLY HAD THEM IN OUR SMALL GROUP FOR TWELVE MONTHS.

WE ONLY SAW THEM WHEN WE DROPPED OFF THEIR MEALS ON TUESDAYS.

WE ONLY KNEW THEIR FAMILY WHILE THEY WERE IN THE MIDDLE OF THE DIVORCE.

WE WERE ONLY THEIR BUDGET VOLUNTEER COUNSELOR FOR 24 MONTHS.

Our paths crossed, we seized an opportunity to help them in some way, but then we have no idea what happened next in their story. Or what happened after that. We don't know how much our volunteering impacted their faith journey, if at all.

THE MAJORITY OF TIME
WE DON'T GET TO HEAR
THE REST OF EACH
PERSON'S FAITH STORY.

But we have a Heavenly Father who sees all of that, and is planning a big reveal for us one day.

In Heaven we will find out the rest of each story, and see how important the part we played was. We'll understand that what we were doing in our volunteer role had long lasting impact in that person's life. You just gotta believe that we are in for some incredible surprises when all of that becomes known.

Not only does our Heavenly Father see everything, He also knows everything we've done along the way as well. The big and the small. He is aware.

He knows about...

ALL OF THE BINS WE ORGANIZED WITH SUPPLIES FOR SUNDAYS

THE LOCK-INS WHERE WE LOST A YEAR'S WORTH OF SLEEP OVER THE YEARS

ALL OF THE REHEARSALS THAT PEOPLE WERE LATE TO AND WE SHOWED UP ON TIME

THE MESSAGES WE PREPARED LATE INTO THE NIGHT

THE CAMPS WE CREATED, ADMINISTRATED, LED, PACKED UP AND SURVIVED

THE EMOTIONAL DRAMA IN YOUR SMALL GROUP

THE SHELTERS WHERE WE SERVED FOOD, COLLECTED COATS, OR RAISED MONEY

THE LIONS THAT GET MADE ONE AT A TIME, MONTH AFTER MONTH, YEAR AFTER YEAR

He is taking note of your time and all of your prep, and is keeping track.

One day, God promises that you'll really be able to see just how worth it everything was. You are not ever going to be sorry you showed up and invested as a volunteer. You will see whose lives were changed on your watch. You'll get a glimpse of the ripple effect that happened in peoples' lives as a result of how you lived yours.

STAY IN IT

We heard a statistic the other day that broke our hearts. It was in an article called "Why So Few Baby Boomers are Volunteering" in *Forbes*.

"The government's annual volunteering in the United States report just came out and I'm disappointed to report that both the number and percentage of Americans age 45 to 64 who volunteered in the 12 months ending September 2012 fell from the previous year." [3]

How much did baby boomer volunteering drop? A lot! Half a million people! Five hundred thousand people dropped out of the volunteering ranks across all segments of service in society. Those aged 45-64 quit volunteering at four times the rate of younger and older age groups. The article's author, Richard Eisenberg, concludes, "Boomers, hang your heads in shame."

Now, this does not include every person in these categories by any means. We know some great folks who are boomers who are still booming, but at large the number is declining.

Maybe part of this is our fault.

Somewhere along the way this idea came into the world and maybe even into the church that older people didn't matter or had nothing to contribute because of their age.

Let's take that a step further, the idea is even out there that if you have been volunteering a long time, that maybe it is time for you to step aside so some new fresh blood can come in and take your place. Kind of a "being put out to pasture" scenario.

We think that nothing could be further from the truth.

The other truth about this is that no matter how long you've served we all are tempted to stop serving at some point. Whether we are too busy, or dealing with work, or homework is piled high, the reasons are there! But we need you to stay in it for the long haul.

Now, if you are a younger volunteer, and new to the game, stay with us here. This is important for you to understand too, for multiple reasons. One, you will be older and tenured someday. Trust us, it happens. And secondly, it is important for you to understand and respect those who have been around longer than you have. These folks have so much wisdom and leadership to spread around. You need to learn from them and take their counsel on the things they have experienced through the years.

Again, this idea is not to be confused with "Replacing Yourself" like we talked about in chapter 6. We all should be replacing ourselves and mentoring others, but it isn't so we can just quit! It is so we move on to something better and grow in our leadership as our age and tenure extends, too.

We want to talk about this because…

We heard a story about a 45-year-old high school small group leader moving on because he felt like he couldn't offer as much as a 25-year-old could.

We heard a story about 60-year-old middle school greeter hang it up because she couldn't keep up with technology and felt like she was falling behind with the times.

We heard a story about a 73-year-old nursery worker who quit because she felt like she didn't fit in with the "younger moms" who were beginning to volunteer.

I (Adam) saw some this happening in our church too, so I approached our pastor for senior adults and asked if I could come into their annual luncheon. He asked me, "What do you want to do that for?" I said, "Because I want to recruit these people to volunteer. They have something to offer, and I want to tap into it."

He was shocked. He replied, "In the Next Gen Ministry?!! If you want to, go ahead. Let me know how it goes!"

So, I went into the luncheon and made my presentation about volunteering, and sure enough, we had three new volunteers sign up from the senior adult ministry, and they love it. They understand that age and tenure only enhance their ability to serve, not deter it. They understand what it means to stay in it, and how important that can be over time.

Like a woman we know, Susan.

Susan embodies this principle better than anyone we know. She is 71 years old. Susan has served in the church her entire life. We met Susan while she was volunteering and she was running the "Church Membership Class." She had been committed to that for over ten years and ran it with excellence. We asked her if she had ever attended a Sunday School class. She said to us, "Please. I don't need to sit in a room and drink coffee with a bunch of people I already know. There is serving to be done!" Now that's quirky!

Susan approached us one day and she said, "I would like to attend the Orange Conference this year." She wasn't even a family ministry volunteer at the time. If you aren't familiar with the Orange Conference, it is the largest family ministry conference in the country and is a pretty rockin' event! And it generally isn't the norm to have 70-year-olds randomly come up and ask us to attend a rock concert. We replied, "We'd love to have you go, but why?" Susan's answer was simple, "I need to find out more about this and how I can invest my time in the next generation." We signed her up.

When we got back from the event we had a great lunch with Susan and how she wanted to get more involved. We asked her what she wanted to do. I'll never forget her response, "I'm organized and can lead others pretty well. What would you like me to do?" We immediately knew she would be a perfect small group coach. Susan took on a new position investing in the lives of those who invest in the lives of kids.

She has been volunteering in different areas of church ministry for almost fifty years, and now she is using those combined gifts to help our next generation ministry shape the next fifty years.

We'll never forget what she said to us on her first day of "officially" volunteering in the elementary department. She said, "Thank you so much for this opportunity. My grandchildren are this age and I can't think of a better place to be."

Susan understands what it means to stay in it. She doesn't want to give up and roll over just because she is getting up there in her years. She still has so much to give.

Do you need to stay in it?

If you have been volunteering for a year and things have been messy…

"I NEED TO FIND OUT MORE ABOUT THIS AND HOW I CAN INVEST MY TIME IN THE NEXT GENERATION." WE SIGNED HER UP.

If you are about to hit the five-year mark and you think, "I need a break"…

If you are a 20-year veteran and you ponder leaving because you aren't cool anymore…

REMEMBER WHAT YOU ARE FIGHTING FOR.

REMEMBER THE CAUSE THAT YOU ARE SERVING.

REMEMBER HOW IMPORTANT THIS IS.

Stay in it. Don't give up!

Be not normal…

"GLENN OVER TIME"

Glenn volunteered as a small group leader with fifth grade boys on Sundays for forty years. He had been impacted by a church leader when he was nine, so he was passionate about that specific age group.

Now, if you have spent any time at all with fifth grade boys, you know that most Sundays were not mountaintop faith-building experiences for Glenn.

MOST OF THE TIME, HE FELT LIKE HE WAS TRYING TO HERD KITTENS BACK IN A BOX.

MOST OF THE TIME, HE WAS PRETTY SURE HIS BOYS LIKED THE DOUGHNUT HOLES HE BROUGHT MORE THAN HIS SMALL GROUP DISCUSSION TIME.

MOST OF THE TIME, HIS BOYS ACTED PAN-PIZZA DEEP EMOTIONALLY AND SPIRITUALLY.

To say that his boys were a work in progress is an understatement. But Glenn knew that. In fact, he remembered very well what it was like to be a nine-year-old boy.

So......

HE SHOWED UP AT SOME OF THEIR SPORTS EVENTS.

HE REMEMBERED THEIR BIRTHDAYS.

HE WROTE THEM NOTES OF ENCOURAGEMENT.

HE CALLED THEIR PARENTS TO CHECK IN WITH THEM FROM TIME TO TIME.

Now Glenn didn't think he was doing anything big or special. But he kept showing up anyway.

Years later, his daughter threw a surprise party for Glenn for his 60th birthday. She invited the church to come after the Sunday service and share some cake with their family as they celebrated their dad.

After the chocolate cake had been served, she asked if anyone wanted to share a story about Glenn. That's when some of the invisible investment Glenn had made over the years started to surface.

A 20-year-old guy was the first one to jump up to the microphone. He thanked Glenn for coming to his basketball games on Saturdays. His own dad had to work on Saturdays and couldn't come to see him play. It had meant the world to him whenever Glenn showed up in the stands cheering for him, even though he had never shown it at the time.

Then a 16-year-old student grabbed the mic and held up a shoebox for all to see. He had read and reread every note that Glenn had ever sent him. He had stored them in that shoebox under his bed. That was the year his sister had been adopted, and Glenn had walked with him through a year of changes that happened to him when she came.

A single mom shared how grateful she had been for Glenn's words of wisdom to her over the phone. She had three sons, and all of them had been in Glenn's group as the years went by. Turns out, Glenn had prayed her through some lonely, tough times. She thanked him because she believed that she was a better mom today because of him.

Story after story. Small and big things, some extremely funny, others wonderfully impactful. It was obvious that Glenn's life had the kind of ripple effect that comes after years of serving in one place.

But, Glenn didn't know any of this. He listened with a sense of awe and wonder as he heard how God had used His life to impact others.

NOTHING HE HAD DONE HAD COST HIM LOTS OF MONEY.

NOTHING HE HAD SAID WAS SUPER-BRILLIANT OR CREATIVE.

HE JUST CARED. HE JUST SHOWED UP.

And he couldn't believe what God had done through his simple service.

Glenn finally stepped up and thanked everyone for coming.

He said the best thing about volunteering was that he always felt like he got back much more than he gave.

"I am the one who has benefitted the most over all of these years."

And then he closed by saying, "See you all next Sunday!"

JUST FOR YOU

Well, we hope we did our best to challenge you to live a life that is more than this world has to offer. We want you to really live life to its fullest.

Be not normal and…

Live like your hair is on fire with a passion to change something for someone else. Jump in and start volunteering somewhere.

Surprise the daylights out of someone else by loving them for free.

Put your head on the pillow at night and feel a sense of fulfillment and purpose that is more than you ever imagined possible.

Get more than you give by owning not renting. Your investment is going to pay off in the end. You will not be sorry when this is all over.

Find a good leader and team up with their vision to take the biggest hill you can climb for Kingdom impact. Pray harder, trust more and grow faster than you ever have before.

Connect with those you volunteer with, so that every week can feel like you are going to a party with your friends. Those friends will make your life richer, and you will have way more fun.

Keep asking who's next and what's next so you don't limit where God can take you in the future. There are so many bright days still up ahead. You don't want to miss one of them.

Remember you can't always see it. It takes time for life change to happen. But if we don't see it here, we have Heaven to look forward to. Stay in it and don't give up.

When you choose to do life with these things in mind, you will not be the same person you are now. We guarantee it.

So, what are you waiting for? "See you next Sunday!" (or whenever and wherever your volunteering takes you.)

WHEN YOU CHOOSE
TO DO LIFE WITH THESE
THINGS IN MIND, **YOU
WILL NOT BE THE SAME
PERSON YOU ARE NOW.**
WE GUARANTEE IT.

1

SCHNAUZERS

Our family has always been in love with schnauzers with floppy ears. And when I say "we" I really just mean me. It started with two salt and pepper miniature schnauzers named Rocky and Smoky. They were fantastic dogs with amazing temperaments. They set the bar for all the schnauzers who came after them. We have had nine more schnauzers after them over the years. We have tried all three sizes of this breed: mini, standard and giant. Number 11 is alive and well right now with us. His name is Wrigley after the stadium where the Chicago Cubs played in our home town. He loves riding on our boat, running in the woods, and chasing the cats up the street.

ICED TEA WITH LOTS OF ICE

This is my favorite drink of choice. I still like it best with a lime added to it, but do not want any sugar in my drink at all. (Sorry Reggie, I really tried to like Sweet Georgia Tea. But at least I like lots of ice like you do!) Besides, I am saving all of my sugar calories up for my piece of daily chocolate.

5

CHOCOLATE

This is my Achilles heal when it comes to calories. I love to have a small amount of chocolate every day if at all possible. Many of the international leaders I have mentored over the years know this about me. When I'm in one of their countries, they surprise me with all kinds of chocolate bars for me to sample. So far, I have not found one that I do not like.

5 QUIRKY THINGS
SUE STUCK WITH

2

MY HUSBAND

He is my best friend, my biggest cheerleader and top encourager. He is a great dad and Papa, and he has put up with 11 schnauzers because of his love for me. I am definitely sticking with him the whole way. We are having so much fun right now as empty nesters. We stay up later than we used to, eat out more than we ever did, and live life at a more relaxed pace on purpose.

3

GYM SHOES

I was standing in the shoe aisle of a large department store trying to figure out what shoes to buy for walking several miles each day. Since I have already had to replace both of my knees with titanium parts, I was looking for great cushioning while on the greenway walking path. A marathon runner happened to be examining shoes too, so I asked her what she recommended. She told me Nike Lunarlon Shoes and showed me why they were so highly rated by marathoners. I grabbed those shoes off the rack and bought them on the spot. And she was so right. They are fantastic shoes! I buy those same shoes every year.

4

5 QUIRKY THINGS
ADAM STUCK WITH

1

PRILOSEC OTC

I had some heartburn one day and tried this 14-day medicine. 14 days?!?! Who wants to take something for that long. Yet, like any consumer in middle class America, we proceed out of marketing compliance. Well, I can happily say, because I stuck with Prilosec OTC I am heartburn free to this day, no matter how many hot peppers I have.

MINISTRY

Many folks have asked me time and time again this question, "Why don't you move to Los Angeles and be an actor or host some show? Why are you doing this church thing?" My answer is simple.

1. I can't memorize dialogue well enough to be an actor.

2. Hosting sounds fun, but what I am doing now is far more important.

Do I think I will be doing what I do now forever? Maybe, maybe not. But I do believe that the local church is the hope of the world, and as long as I am able, I want to devote my time, energy, and passion into helping families understand that. However, both Ryan Seacrest and Carson Daly need to watch themselves should I ever decide to pursue the alternative.

5

FORT LAUDERDALE

I love this town. When I moved to South Florida from a little town called Temperance, Michigan, I thought to myself, "There is no way I will be here long. This place is too diverse, too obsessed with what's hot, and too 'Miami' for me." Turns out, I'm a little that way too. It is the "Venice of America" with more waterways than streets and has become my home. From the restaurants, to the night life, from the ocean to the people, I love every moment of being in one of my favorite places.

NOT WEARING SOCKS

Not wearing socks is extremely classy. People make fun of me all the time and will ask me why I am not wearing socks. I just say, "Check any fashion magazine or blog and tell me if anyone is wearing socks." Plus my friend Mike reminds me that not wearing socks saves on washing 730 fewer things every year. It's for the environment! I'm sticking to it, even if some of my shoes do smell like my grandfather's restroom after the annual Thanksgiving feast.

SURVIVOR

That's right, the 15-year-old reality show that changed television forever. I still watch each and every episode, no matter how old the show gets. It was one of those revolutionary pieces of television that altered the course of history. I have applied to be on the show about two dozen times and made it to the semi-final interviews in 2004 but didn't make the cast. One of these days, though...and I'll need you to help keep me on the island.

[1]   Seinfeld, "The Old Man," February 18, 1993, Season 4, Episode 18

[2]   So technically, the word "privately" isn't in that exact translation since the venerable Eugene Peterson says "just between the two of you." But nearly every other translation uses the word "privately," and we like it here. To Peterson's credit (and he deserves a lot of credit), his translation of the word is probably better than all those other versions, since those other translations combine five different Greek words into the one word "privacy," whereas the key word in the phrase metaxy combines with the other four to literally mean *"just between us."* Just like Peterson said.

[3]   Richard Eisenberg, "Why So Few Baby Boomers are Volunteering," *Forbes Magazine*, http://www.forbes.com/sites/ nextavenue/2013/04/01/can-we-get-some-volunteers-please/, accessed 26 November 2014

ACKNOWLEDGMENTS

It might seem normal for us to thank all of the volunteers who have worked with us through the years, but we are going to do it anyway. Without those who have served with us through the years, we would have had no stories to tell, mistakes to laugh about, wisdom to pass along, or victories to celebrate. So, thank you!

We would also like to thank a few other people...

Reggie Joiner. For giving us the opportunity to write this book that we are so passionate about. You have stuck through us through every creative twist and turn and were able to guide the 30,000-feet flyover process for this project better than anyone we have ever seen. We would also like to thank you for encouraging us to change the title and direction of the book once we were halfway done with it. That is just not normal! But wow, what a difference it made. Especially in our holiday plans. Kidding, Reg! We love ya!

Goldendoodles Incorporated of America. For encouraging Springview Mini Goldendoodles in Orlando to produce a litter that went home September 27, 2014, so Dottie Duckworth could join the Duckworth Family. Without Dottie by our side, we aren't sure how we would have written this book. She reminded us that being Not Normal is the best thing ever! Because she is an extremely Not Normal dog.

Mike Jeffries. Our editor. How could we have done this without you and your consistent feedback? If we could express our appreciation on paper we would, but you'd probably edit what we say and say what you wanted to say anyway.

Additionally we would like to thank Lois, Katelyn, Rick, Amy, Matt, Steak954 on Fort Lauderdale Beach, and everyone else who helped us craft our content along the way.

Individually...

Adam would like to thank Barb Baird. Barb was the first volunteer who ever came alongside him and is one of his dearest friends and mentors to this very day.

Sue would like to thank Pat Cimo, her co-leader at Willow for so many years. Pat is an incredible leader of volunteers, and one of the best friends Sue ever had.

ABOUT THE AUTHORS

SUE MILLER

Sue is a teacher, leader, speaker, and author with a passion for bringing out the best in volunteers. Much of that passion developed over the 17 years she served as Children's Ministry Director at Willow Creek Community Church near Chicago, Illinois. Her ongoing challenge was to figure out how to recruit, grow, and keep a fantastic team of volunteers that could influence the faith of the 3,000 kids that attended each weekend. She also served on the senior management team under the leadership of pastor Bill Hybels, a champion of volunteerism.

In 2005, Sue joined Orange, a nonprofit organization that creates resources to help churches partner with parents to build faith in the next generation. She's traveled all over the world helping parents and churches develop life-changing experiences for children and teenagers.

Currently she and Adam work with a team to create Live to Serve conferences. These are one-day training events for volunteers that are creative, informative, and impactful (fun too!) Sue is the author of several books, including *Parenting Is Wonder-full* and *Making Your Children's Ministry the Best Hour of Every Kid's Week*.

When not working, Sue lives with her handsome husband, Rick, in a fixer-upper house in Atlanta, Georgia. She does life with her two favorite adult kids, one amazing son-in-law, a mischievous black mini schnauzer and two of the most incredible grandsons on the planet.

ADAM DUCKWORTH

Adam Duckworth is the Family Pastor at First Fort Lauderdale, a forward-thinking downtown church committed to reaching families and embracing culture in its community. First Fort Lauderdale is at the center of South Florida's fastest-growing business, entertainment and residential corridor midway between Miami and Palm Beach. Members of the church come from more than 70 different nations, giving a completely new meaning to "family tradition."

Before launching a career of leading volunteers at a church, Adam attended the University of Toledo, where he completed degrees in both education and English.

In addition to leading Live to Serve with Sue Miller, Adam hosts the Studio 252 program and serves as a communicator at Camp KidJam, Orange Conference and Orange Tour.

At First Fort Lauderdale, Adam has revolutionized the volunteer culture by creating opportunities for volunteers to serve, leading them toward a common goal, and leveraging the influence of the next generation to volunteer as well.

Adam lives a block from the beach in Fort Lauderdale with his wife, Katelyn, and their petite goldendoodle, Dottie. For more information about Adam, follow him on Twitter @adam_duckworth.